The Power of the Bull

Inside the Head of Sculptor Wayne Porter

The Story of Porter Sculpture Park

Sue Speck

An inspiring book about the audacity and tenacity it took for a small town, self-taught metal artist to propel himself from obscurity to national and international acclaim by creating his own sculpture park on the prairie.

An authorized biography

The Power of the Bull

Inside the Head of Sculptor Wayne Porter

The Story of Porter Sculpture Park

ISBN 979-8-9925997-5-6

The photography is also by Sue Speck, except for Porter family photos, which are used with permission from Wayne Porter.

Poems and excerpts are also used with the permission of Wayne Porter.

Printed in the United States of America.

This book is dedicated to my parents,
who were among Wayne's
earliest believers and
who always believed in me.

Table of Contents

"Art is

thought made tangible."

Wayne Porter

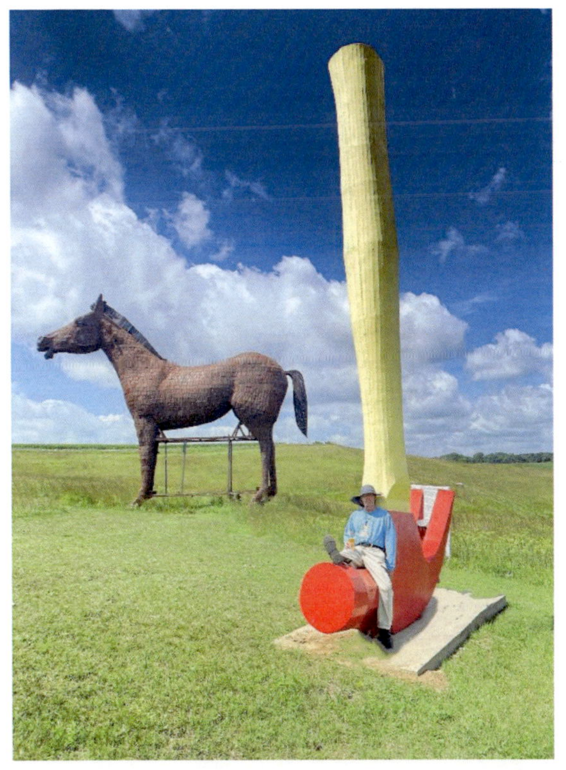

Wayne Porter sitting on his hammer sculpture

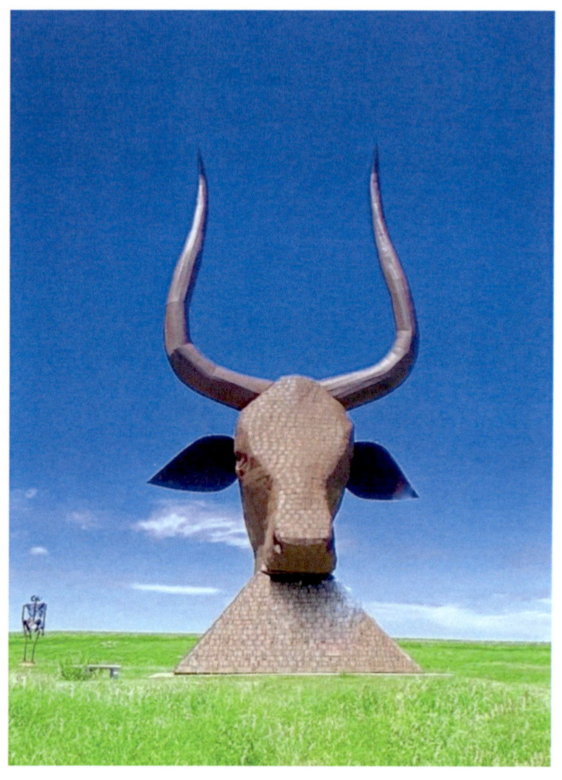

"The Bull"
is as tall as the faces on Mount Rushmore.

Origins

Some things command inexplicable power.

The power of an ethereal sunset, the power of the rising sun aligning perfectly to create a golden halo around the head of a sculpture, the power of a massive bull's head suddenly appearing on the horizon along an interstate highway.

The power of the bull is manifested in history with ancient civilizations from the cave dwellers to the Bronze Age Minoans honoring the muscular bovine's strength in their art to modern America's charging bull sculpture on Wall Street symbolizing optimism and prosperity.

It's the same power that Wayne Porter was drawn to from the time he was a child, before he launched himself to national and international attention as a metal artist with a multi-story tall bull as a centerpiece in his sculpture park on the prairie.

And it all started with a bull that fits in the palm of your hand.

Formation

Wayne Porter discovered his power to create in the most likely and unlikely of places.

Likely, because it was in the middle of cattle country where bulls were part of the scenery. Unlikely, because there weren't any artists or art around his little town as far as he could see.

Wayne grew up as the middle child of a nurse and a farmer-turned-blacksmith in St. Lawrence, South Dakota, where farmers and ranchers depended on an ironsmith who could bend and weld metal for their farm equipment.

Aside from the sculptures Wayne has made there, the biggest attraction is St. Lawrence Natural Park, which is just as the name implies: a no-frills, but scenic park surrounded by elm trees and hackberry trees along Turtle Creek with a red community hall that resembles an old-fashioned barn.

Fish and crawdads swim in the stream and squirrels scamper in the trees, where branches bend and twist into intricate shapes, forming abstract shadows and reflections, an ideal atmosphere to stoke the imagination of a little boy.

Deer take shelter in the trees on the hills of the park and roam the quiet streets of the town in the middle of the night, grazing in the yards of home owners and searching for kernels of grain and corn in the commercial grain elevator and storage bins.

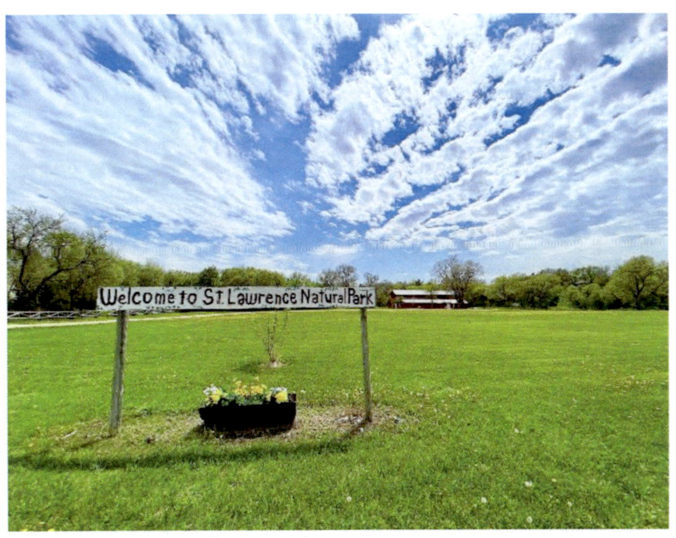

St. Lawrence Natural Park

In the 1960's when Wayne was a child, this community of less than 200 people boasted a school, a restaurant, a hotel, bar, gas station, a church and a general store where you could buy candy for a penny.

For a youngster, the town was quintessential Americana, an unspoiled place to climb the park hills, ride bikes, watch for trains at the trestle bridge and wave at the train engineers who waved and blew their whistles in return, the beginning of a relationship with the railroad that would factor heavily into Wayne's future.

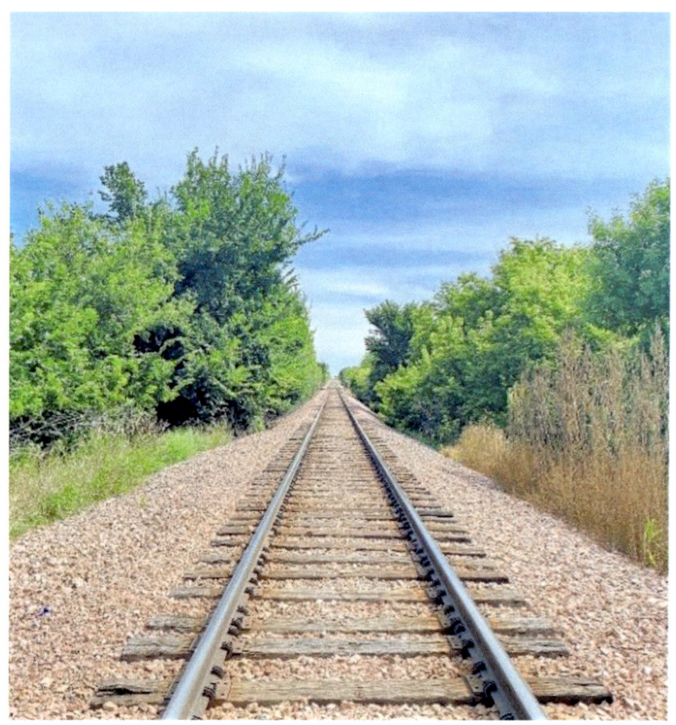

The railroad tracks in St. Lawrence

"It was fun. We grew up free range," Wayne recalls. "We could run all over town, but we couldn't cross Highway 14 because there was traffic. We were told to be home when the street lights came on. We were free range kids."

"We didn't know there was evil. We didn't know bad things were happening out there."

Wayne's backyard bordered Turtle Creek. After a snowy Midwestern winter, the stream can swell and burst beyond its banks, dragging fragments of whatever was near enough to the water to be swept along into its current.

For a child with ingenuity and an aptitude for building, it was a bonanza.

Debris floating on the water became building blocks for the boy who would become a nationally and internationally known sculptor.

"Barn doors would float down on the creek so I would make rafts out of them," Wayne said.

While the creek may have provided a source of entertainment for Wayne as a child, his use of salvaged material from the stream set a natural precedent for using recycled scrap material in his future sculptures.

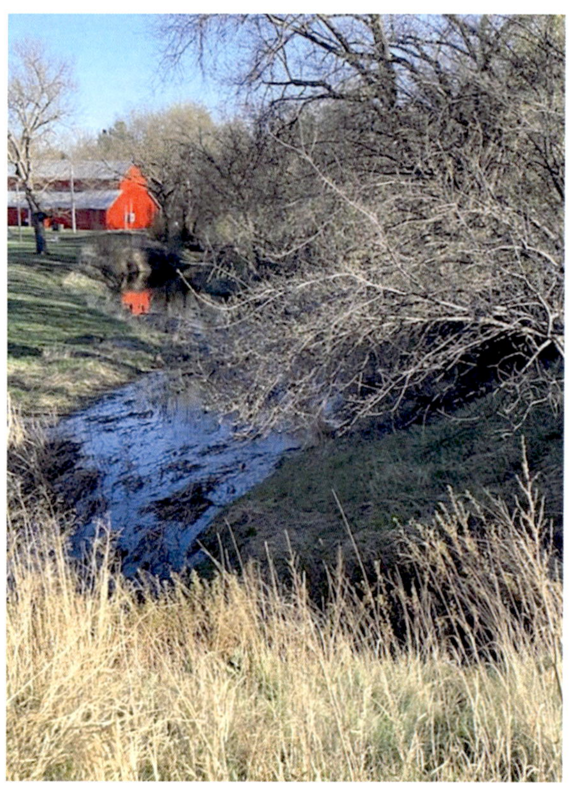

Turtle Creek in early spring just after the snow has melted and as the leaves are budding.

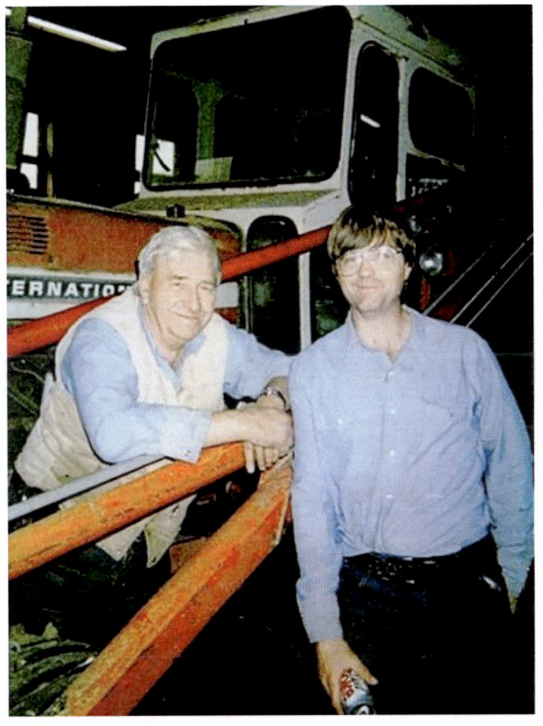

Wayne and his father Gene Porter.
Gene was the town blacksmith.
Photo courtesy of Wayne Porter

Wayne spent much of his time at his father Gene's almost century old blacksmith shop, learning welding skills from his dad and helping him create repairs for the rural community. He started welding for customers before he was a teen-ager.

"Farm kids start working early," he said. "We're recruited from the crib."

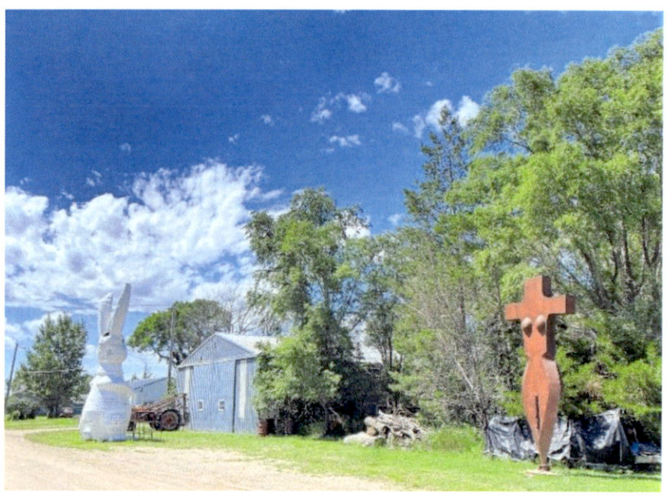

The blacksmith shop with two sculptures: the "White Rabbit" and "The Blade."

The blacksmith shop was also a gathering spot where farmers would stop to chat. He listened to the adults talk about cattle, the crops, the farm economy and politics, all which would be woven into his future work.

He discovered that some of the farmers were also old soldiers, some of whom had served in World War II, which was only about a quarter century in the past at that point.

Their war stories were his first glimpse into an imperfect world outside of his sheltered environment and into personal stories about history from people he knew.

He not only developed an appreciation for history; he also developed a reverence for the veterans and their courage.

"These old people would come in and they'd talk about World War II. Some of these people really went through a lot," he said. "I appreciate it a lot more now."

A Journey Begins

As he heated metal to red hot temperatures and manipulated it with a hammer on his father's anvil and metal press, Wayne discovered that the practical metal work that was essential for farm equipment could be transformed into beautiful and fantastical shapes.

His first attempt at metal art was a miniature bull's head.

He used a cutting torch and a grinder to form it from scrap metal, solid and heavy. There was no one to tell the 10-year-old that sculptures are often not solid, but are hollow, made from a mold.

He prizes the rudimentary piece as his first work.

"It was thick steel. I'm very proud of it," he said. "It was kind of lopsided."

Wayne fashioned the diminutive bull's head into a pendant and wore it around his neck for years. In a sense, he'd branded himself as an artist even though he wasn't conscious of his talent.

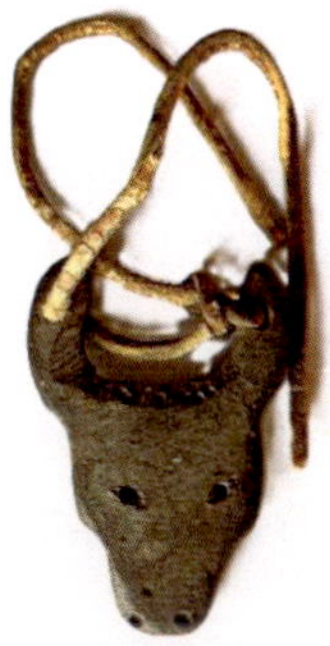

Wayne made his first bull sculpture at age 10.

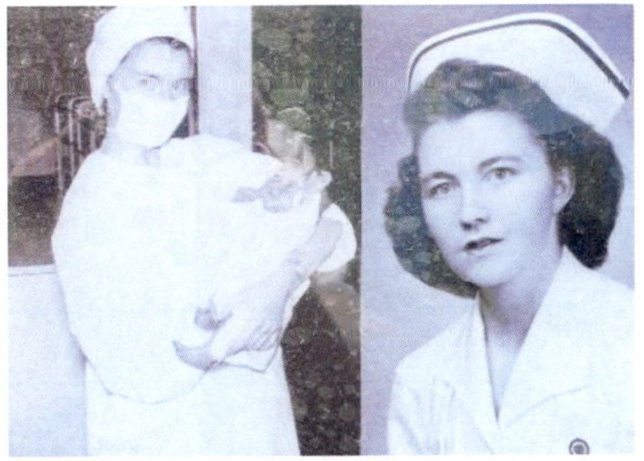

Wayne's mother
Photo courtesy of Wayne Porter

His mother was. Mary Ellen Rudd Porter told her son early on that he was an artist and encouraged his creative curiosity. She was a nurse who wrote poetry in her youth and had an appreciation for the visual, beautifying the community by planting marigold flowers around town.

But central South Dakota in those days wasn't the kind of place that cultivated culture.

Art classes in elementary school centered largely on coloring and cutting and pasting, instructed by the teacher who taught all subjects to the class.

If it was limited exposure to art, it may also have been liberating and contributed to Wayne's lack of inhibitions in his approach to his artwork.

No expectations can equal no boundaries.

"All kids are artists," Wayne said. "But they're told it isn't pretty enough. The lines don't look right, people aren't pink or purple, and they stop. There is a natural gravity toward normal."

"I never cared. I didn't care. I didn't call it art. I just had fun. I didn't see it as art. I was imagining stories in my head and made the stories become real."

Wayne found books at the Hand County Library that began his literary journey into the world of art, learning and teaching himself about history and culture outside his small town.

"I'd look at these art books. I'd look at these books and think, 'people really do this.' The Hand County library is my teacher."

He progressed from the bull pendant to making miniature animal sculptures out of bronze.

His first step beyond miniatures was a foot tall sculpture of a horse made with molten bronze through a drip by drip, drop by drop process, again heavy and solid, and an animal reflective of his surroundings.

When he was a teenager, Wayne made a condor with a wingspan of eight feet that was inspired by the vultures that soar in the skies above the prairie. This time, he used tin, a metal much lighter and more malleable than bronze.

His use of tin made him aware of the possibilities of infinite shapes on a larger scale with more flexible metal, but his sculptures at that point were still largely reflective of his surroundings and what he observed.

"Your place organizes a lot of your thoughts," Wayne said. "The culture where you're from is hard wired into you. You can't really get rid of it even if you try. You're still going to be that person."

Rejection

Even as he enjoyed creating, art was still just an interest, a hobby, not something he planned to pursue as his life's work. In fact, he resisted the idea that he could spend his life as an artist.

A distant great uncle on his mother's side was artistic, but his immediate family was more technical and scientific. His older brother and sister went into medicine, his younger brother became a mechanical engineer, and his younger sister became a microbiologist.

When it was time for college, Wayne's mother suggested that he major in art, but Wayne had other ideas, primarily because he didn't know anybody who was making a living from art.

And there's a difference between making art and making a living off it.

"You've heard of starving artists," Wayne said. "I wanted food. You can't eat paint."

Wayne chose what he considered a more sensible career and started college at South Dakota State

University in Brookings, South Dakota, as a biology major.

His discomfort with dissections changed his direction though, and he switched his focus to political science and history, interests influenced by the discussions he heard as a child at the blacksmith shop.

Each course of study finds its way into his art today, including biology with a sculpture of a dissection of a frog and a poem serving as commentary on the post-mortem process.

In his "Buzzard Row" series, based on historical events, the sculptures represent scavenger vultures lying in wait and holding dining forks as well as tools such as axes, hammers and mallets. The birds have metal bibs around their necks in anticipation of dinner.

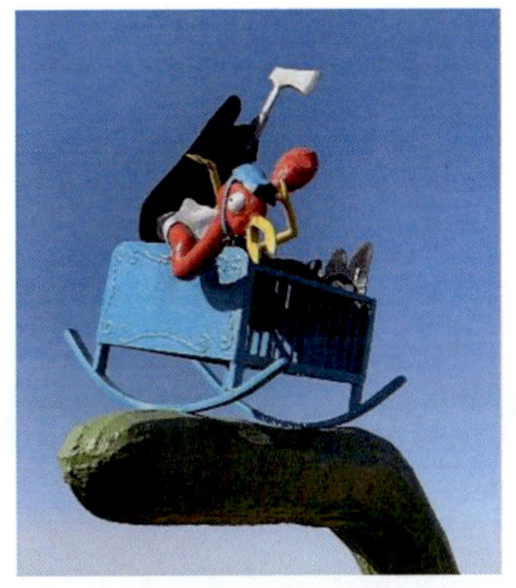

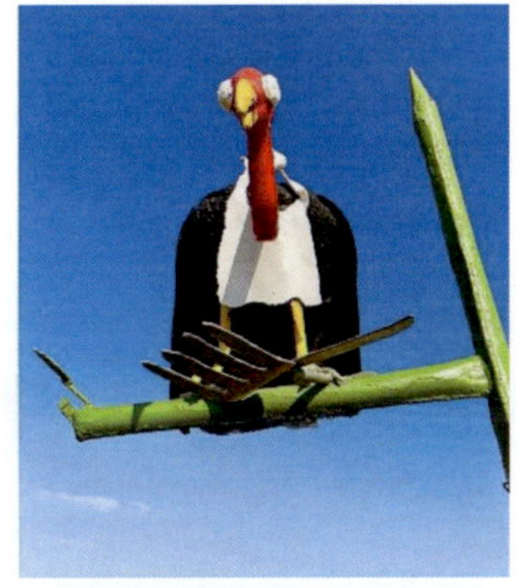

The details in the buzzard sculptures include forks, bibs, hatchets and hammers.

His background in history provided an academic and historical context not just for the buzzard series, but also for his understanding of the importance and symbolism of the bull throughout history.

In college, Wayne concentrated on his major and actively avoided art classes as electives.

"I didn't want anything to do with art classes. The idea of college is not to starve. I did not want the art thing to overtake me."

Summers during college were spent back in St. Lawrence, working at the blacksmith shop and doing what he had been avoiding: art.

He continued to make miniature animal sculptures and then moved on to his first full-sized dragon, a small to medium sized work he describes as crude, but a piece that was a change in technique that would change his life.

He wouldn't recognize it as a pivotal moment until later.

"That's where I developed the style," Wayne said.

His summer fun was still just fun, but he was enjoying metal artistry so much and finding it so natural that he was beginning to wonder if there could be a purpose for his creativity and if he could actually earn some income from his talent.

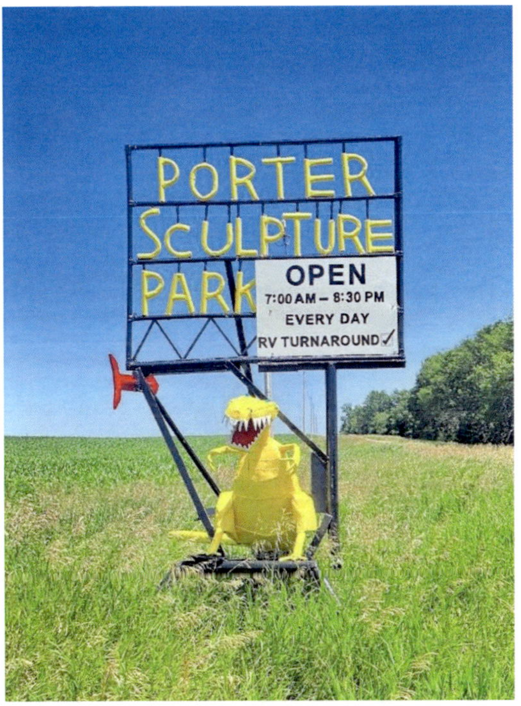

Wayne's first dragon sculpture now serves as part of the sign to his sculpture park.

But first, the practical. After graduation, he couldn't escape the common sense mentality that was so much part of his Midwestern upbringing.

He considered law school and was accepted at the University of South Dakota Law School, but decided it was too expensive and he wasn't the lawyerly type anyway. So he went home to think about his next move.

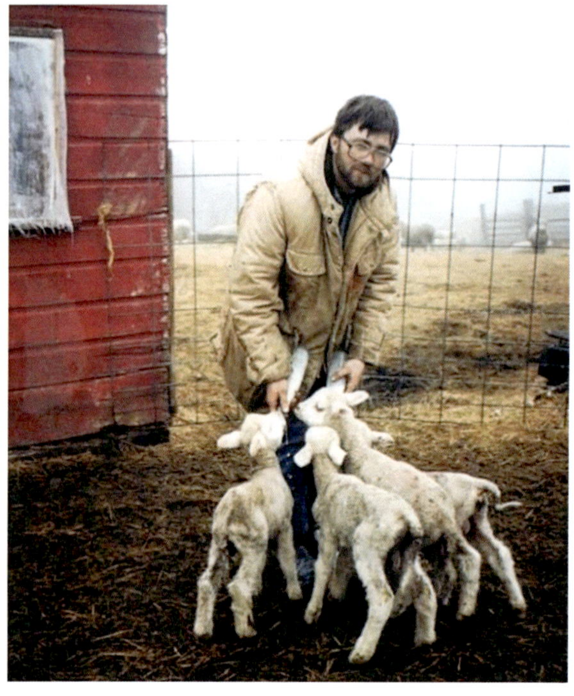

Wayne Porter bottle feeding lambs in the 1980's.
He was a sheep rancher and blacksmith
before he became a full-time artist.
Photo courtesy of Wayne Porter

Wayne began working at the blacksmith shop with his dad and raising sheep. He was a watchful shepherd, protecting his flock in blizzards in winter and bottle feeding struggling lambs in the spring.

It fulfilled the independent side of him and gave him the creative space for his imaginative side to fully emerge.

“I didn’t like the idea of working for someone. I like to daydream and there aren’t a whole lot of jobs like that,” he said.

“Watching sheep graze was a pretty nice place, but I needed a place to daydream.”

Obsession

In the summer months when his sheep and goats grazed on their own, he made more sculptures.

The 12-foot-tall red dragon that was his first large sculpture was created the summer after he graduated from college in 1983.

The red dragon became known as the "Magic Dragon" in St. Lawrence because some couples brought along a diamond ring when they visited and became engaged to be married while standing underneath the sculpture.

More dragons as well as dinosaurs followed, evolving from fierce stances to include gentler poses such as "Smell the Roses While You Can" featuring a dinosaur that resembles a Tyrannosaurus rex smelling flowers.

That it might be an implausible juxtaposition for a giant with huge jaws strong enough to crush a car was fully his intention.

"Why not?" Wayne said. "I was having fun. I was goofing off. Art can be fun. It can feel like you're goofing off."

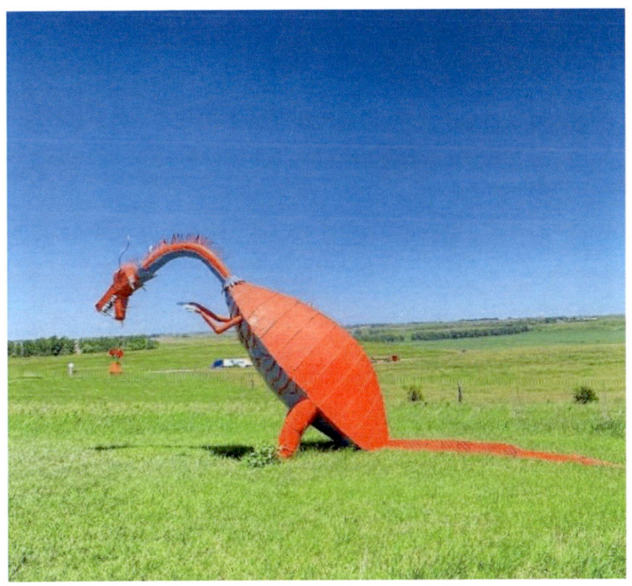

The Red Dragon/Magic Dragon was Wayne's first large sculpture.

He created "Smell the Roses While You Can" after his father told him to cut up the old family station wagon for scrap metal. The hindquarters and flanks of the dinosaur are made from the car's bumper with the original license plate welded onto it.

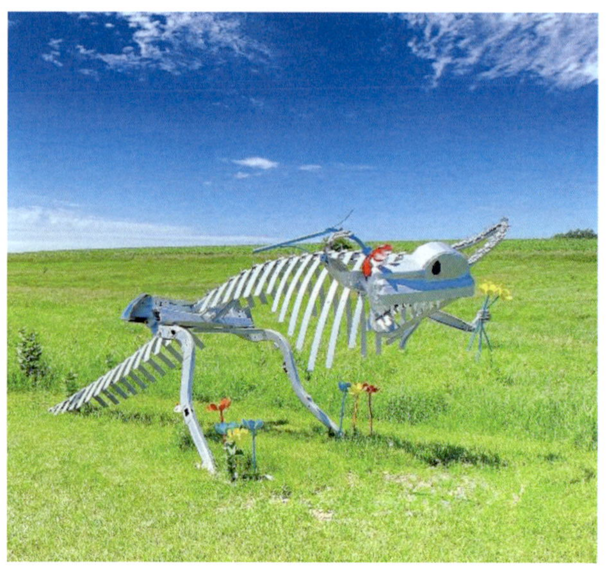

"Smell the Roses While You Can"
depicts a dinosaur smelling flowers.
It and the Red Dragon/Magic Dragon
were among Wayne's earliest sculptures.

Other early sculptures were a mixture of whimsical and fanciful. He captured the thrill of a child sledding down a hill, based on his childhood experience sledding down the snow packed hills of St. Lawrence Park in winter, screaming as he sped down a particularly treacherous slope.

"There's a hill called Dead Man's Hill. It's a really steep slope. I went down it once. It was not a smart move," he said. "But I survived."

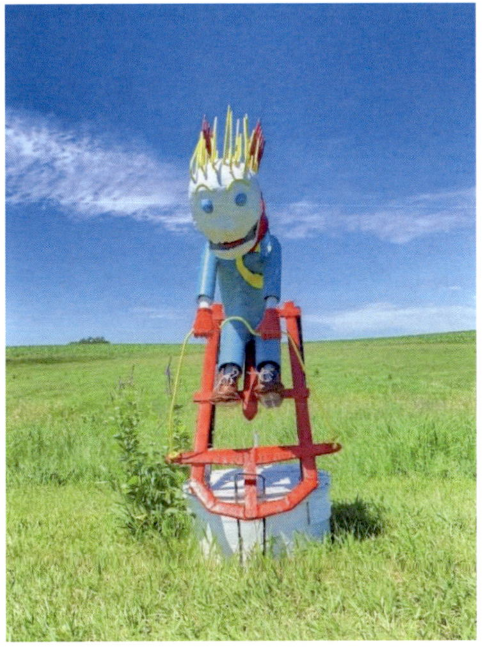

"Dead Man's Hill" is made with antique sled runners.

Wayne used other personal experiences as inspiration as well, turning one bad experience into a sculpture of a wasp holding a fly swatter. He created "The Wasp" after a painful encounter with a nest of yellow jacket wasps.

"Until the swelling went down, all I could think of was yellow jackets. Then I found this antique refrigerator compressor and I thought it looked like a wasp's head so that's where this comes from."

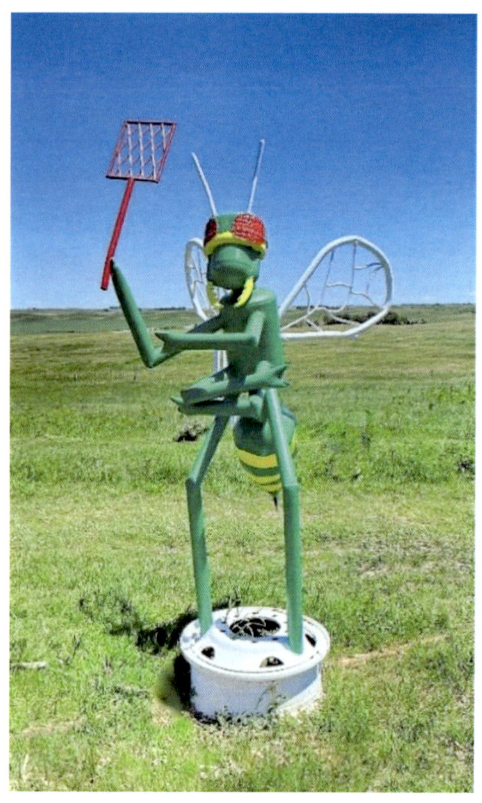

"The Wasp"
The fly swatter and the wings
are made of expanded metal,
which is a webbed metal.

To make his sculptures, he initially used scraps from his father's shop, recycled materials from Turtle Creek, and items from the town junk yard, which proved to be a treasure trove of material. He found discarded household items including old water heaters and creamers from milk and butter making.

The "Miss Muppet and the Spider" sculpture was created using a creamer as the body of the spider and springs from farm machinery for the curly hair.

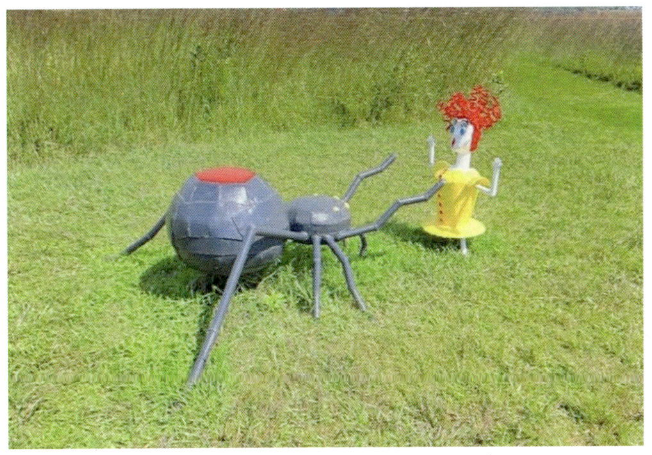

"Miss Muppet and the Spider"

Farmers' obsolete and inoperable equipment provided cultivator shovels, sickle sections from mowers, chisel points from plows, roller chains from feed wagons, antique buggy axels from pioneer day transportation, and semi-truck parts from modern trucks. What Wayne couldn't find, he created, welded together from raw metal.

Some works were inspired by his flock. The goat in his "Goat Playing a Saxophone" sculpture was painted the same color as one of his billy goats. He later added dancers dangling flowers around the musical goat, calling the entire scene "The Spring-Autumn Festival."

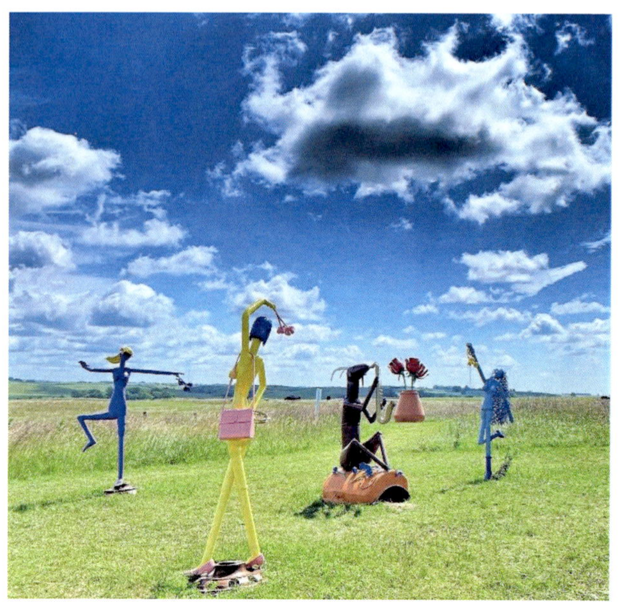

"The Spring-Autumn Festival" features his "Goat Playing a Saxophone" with dancers around it.

His Jack in the Box sculpture, titled "Jack in Pandora's Box" was created during a time when he was reading horror novels.

"I just made it a little more scary than it should have been. I was reading Stephen King stuff. I'm a hot pepper guy. I spice things up so the early stuff can be a bit scary. I don't want to do anything that bores me so I crank it up."

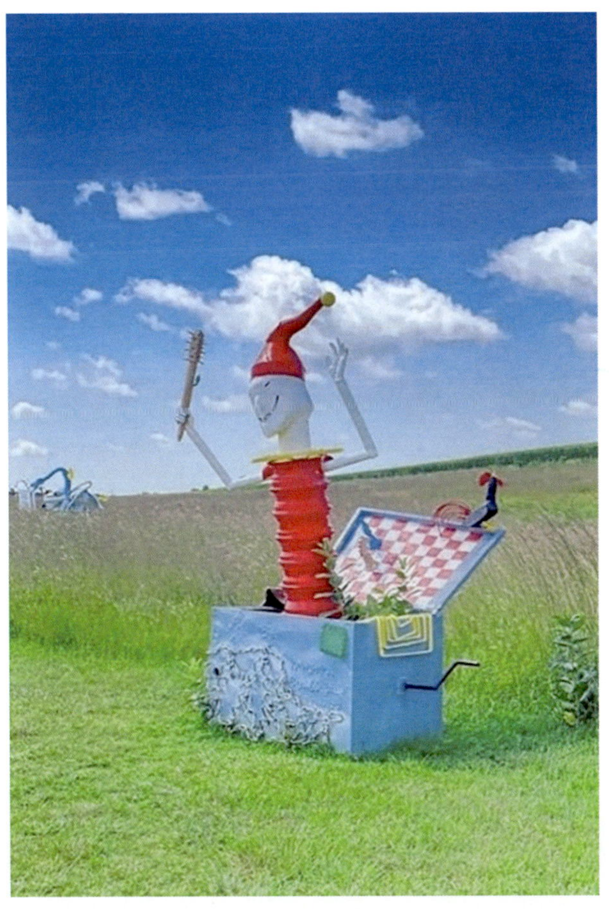

"Jack in Pandora's Box"

"Jack in Pandora's Box" contains complexities in the significance of the details. The yellow on the side of the box signifies the evil that escaped into the world after the box was opened. The rooster signifies that a new morning has begun.

The chess board is symbolic of the importance of knowing how to play the game of life, an unbalanced game in Pandora's box.

"The chess pieces are in a position so the game can't be won," Wayne said.

The club in the hand appears ominous studded with spikes, but all is not lost in Wayne Porter's Pandora's box. A closer look reveals a glimmer of light among the hard, harsh spikes: one single, gentle leaf.

"Hope is a leaf on the club," Wayne said.

And an emotion he would soon find in great demand in his community.

As the farm economy faltered during the 1980's, a serious, personal tone emerged in his work.

The talk at the blacksmith shop turned to the struggles farmers were facing due to drought, poor crops, falling land values, debt and high interest rates.

The 1980's farm crisis, which put thousands of farmers out of business, was the worst economic downturn in the agricultural community since the Great Depression in 1929 and the 1930's.

Wayne paid homage to his rural neighbors in a poem and a sculpture by creating his poignant "American Gothic - Shepherd's Dream" representing the heartbreak of rural families who were losing their farms during the economic crisis.

The poem speaks of drought reducing fertile soil to dust and the grass that animals eat dying and giving way to drought opportunistic thistles.

At first glance, the sculpture appears to be one of Wayne's simplest pieces, but the depth is evident in the details.

He sculpted what he heard and what he saw in farmers' efforts to hold onto their land and their livelihood, capturing their emotions in words and cold steel, capturing pain so deep that they have been pushed past the point of shedding tears and into stony countenance.

In his sculpture, a farmer stands with his head down. A small house stands at his feet. The hands tell the story of desperation.

"One hand reaches for anything. The other is holding tight to the pitchfork and he's surrounded by barbed wire. He's trapped," explains Wayne.

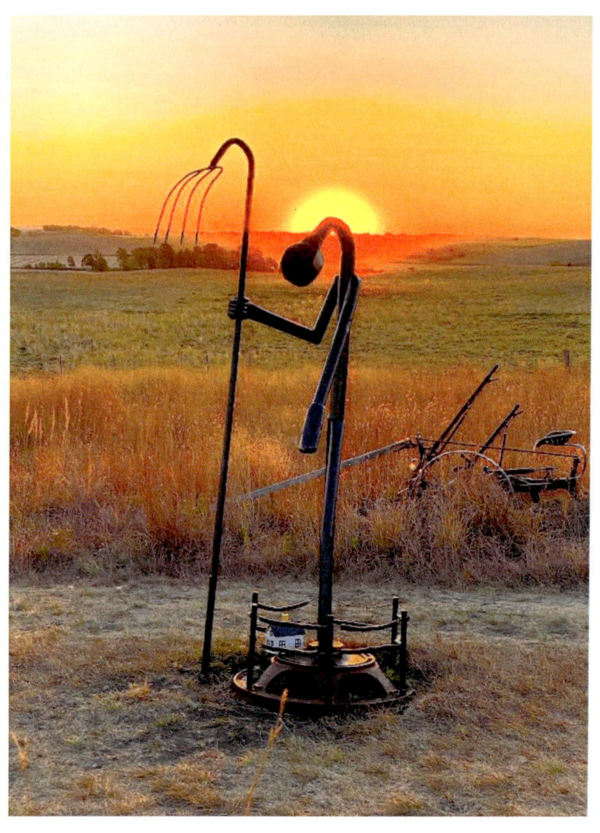

"American Gothic – Shepherd's Dream" farmer sculpture at sunrise. It's a tribute to farm families as they struggled in the 1980's farm crisis.

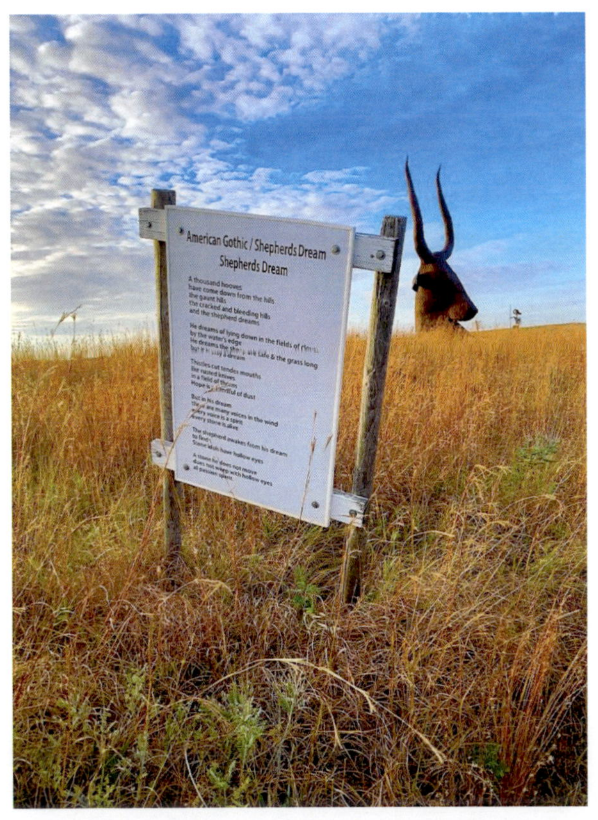

The "American Gothic – Shepherd's Dream" poem was inspired by farmers who lost their land and homes in the 1980's farm crisis.

American Gothic – Shepherd's Dream
by Wayne Porter

A thousand hooves
have come down from the hills
the gaunt hills
the cracked and bleeding hills
and the shepherd dreams

He dreams of lying down in the fields and
by the water's edge
He dreams the sheep are safe & the grass long
but it is only a dream

Thistles cut tender mouths
like rusted knives
in a field of thorns
Hope is a handful of dust

But in his dream
there are many voices in the wind
every voice is a spirit
every stone is alive

The shepherd awakes from his dream
to find
Stone idols have hollow eyes

A stone he does not move
does not weep with hollow eyes
all passion spent.

His work had moved from childhood inspirations to a greater degree of depth and empathy.

"Art is a diary of where the artist was at the time," Wayne said. "Your work of art is your biography. That is who you are in your brain. Art is thought made tangible."

More serious and refined sculptures began emerging, including a rugged, but at once graceful and elegant dusty gold sculpture of a woman kneeling with a broom and a dust pan in her hands.

It weaves together an imaginary story of a maid who cleans a theatre, scrubbing the floor where the ballerinas dance and where the maid dances after they leave at night, wishing she could be a ballerina.

A closer look at the sculpture reveals that there are pieces missing from her body, a parallel to the pieces missing from her life.

The process of picking up the pieces and placing them in the bucket is both a literal and figurative reference to the process of cleaning and the process of living our lives.

"The Ballerina" is a metaphor about the choices we make and what we do with where we are.

"For every choice you make, there are others that you throw away," Wayne said.

"She dreams about being a ballerina. It's about the decisions we make in our lives. She's picking up the pieces of her life and putting them back together."

"The Ballerina" is made, in part, of car leaf springs and the broom is made from welding rods. The base is a 300-gallon barrel that Wayne used as a watering trough for his sheep and the bucket is one he used to feed struggling lambs.

All were parts of his own life coming together to create his new life as an artist.

"The Ballerina" is a favorite of visitors at the sculpture park and not just because of the haunting beauty of the sculpture. It's extraordinarily relatable.

It resonates with anyone who has ever had to re-evaluate any portion of their life. And who hasn't at one time or another?

And it certainly resonates with anyone who has had to pick up many pieces of their life or has known someone in that situation.

To some observers, it's a visual reminder to just keep picking up the pieces. To just keep trying until the missing parts and the ragged edges come back together again.

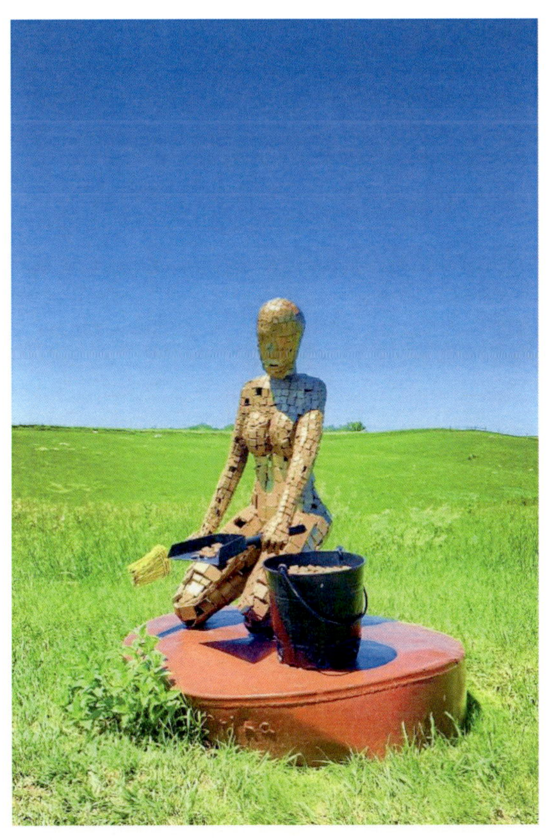

"The Ballerina" is a metaphor for the choices we make in life.

His change in style and the narrative that went with it wasn't an orchestrated change.

The ballerina concept seemed to emerge as a random idea produced in the mind of a developing and maturing artist, or as Wayne puts it, "All thoughts begin in your subconscious, but very few unconscious thoughts make it to the conscious."

Regardless of the reason, his choices of sculptures had become more intentional and thoughtful in terms of story-telling and commentary. He'd also reached a point where art had overtaken both his conscious and subconscious, constantly feeding him ideas.

"Art would wake me up in the middle of the night. The art would haunt me in the middle of the night and wake me up at 2 o'clock in the morning."

That's exactly what happened the night he decided to create a sculpture based on Greek antiquity and fertility figures in history.

"It came to me in a dream," Wayne said. "I woke up at 2 o'clock in the morning and I jotted down the idea."

Two sculptures emerged as a result of his decision to include Greek influences in his work.

"The Floating Muse" was his modern take on classical antiquity using sheet metal welded together instead of carved marble as the ancients used.

"It looks like it's made of balloons," Wayne explains. "Like she's made of balloons and she's floating away."

At first, the muse was painted silver to resemble a floating cloud. Years later, it was changed to vibrant blue, patterned after the color that the French artist Henri Matisse often used for his collages during his cut-out period and reminiscent of Yves Klein blue.

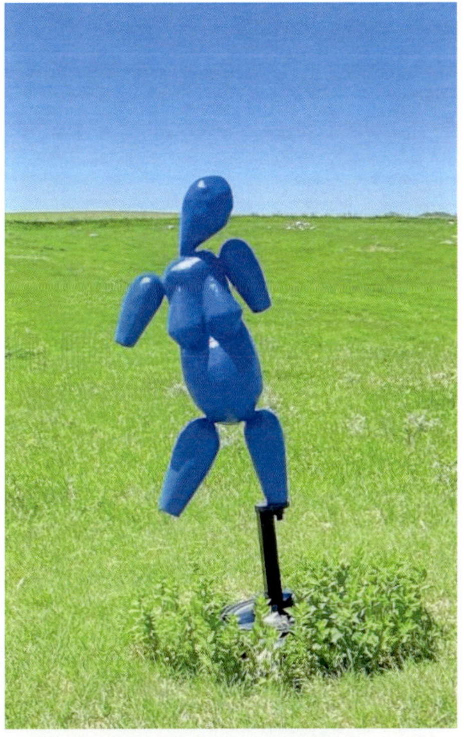

"The Floating Muse"

The hand and head sculpture "The Thought" is essentially a visualization of inspiration and was based on the process of ideas popping out of Wayne's head and into his hands to create art.

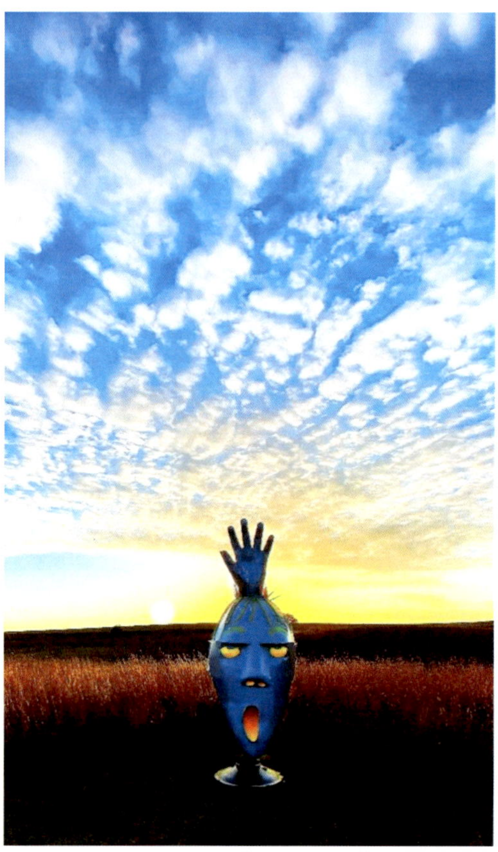

"The Thought" sculpture at sunset in the fall against a backdrop of clouds. The ever-changing sky is part of the experience at Porter Sculpture Park.

After initially resisting it, Wayne now fully acknowledged and embraced his obsession to create. He realized it was just part of his essence.

"I tried to avoid art. It did not work. I was born an artist. I couldn't stop doing it even when I tried to not do it. I'm an artist and that's what it is."

He found that he loved not only creating, but he loved talking about his artwork with people who stopped by the blacksmith shop.

As with all art, not everyone in town liked his sculptures, but they paid attention to them, which, in itself, can be one indicator of the reach and influence of artwork.

Art evokes emotions, whatever those emotions are.

But as more and more pieces began popping up around the blacksmith shop in St. Lawrence, virtually all the locals began asking what Wayne was going to do with all those sculptures and by the time he was 23, the artist knew the answer: he was going to develop his own sculpture park someday.

An audacious decision for a young man who had never taken an art class.

I know what the wind whispers
to the grass
Come to me
Come to me
for I have touched the moon
and I ride on the backs of dragons

Wayne Porter
from his poem
"The Daydreamers"

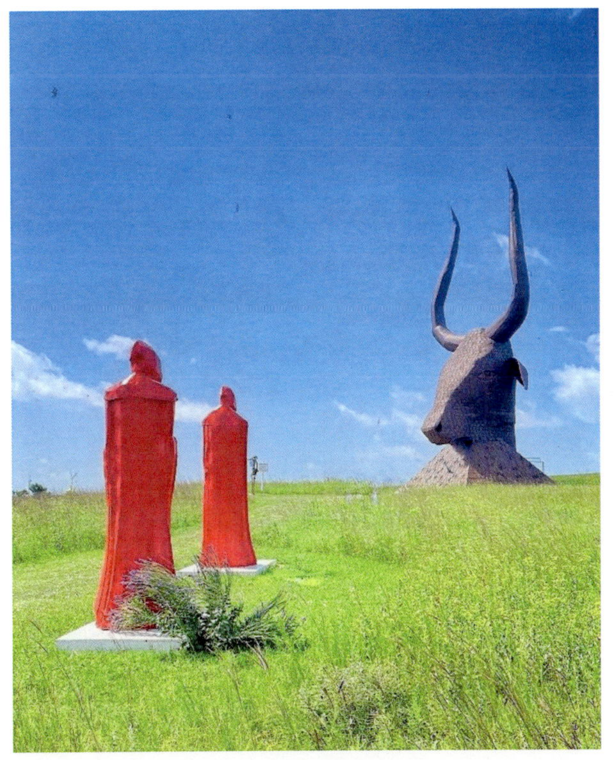

The Monks and the Bull

With the wind in your hair
breathe the night air
Cherish your scars
dream of the stars
almost there.

Wayne Porter
from his poem
"The Wild Ride"

Art as Business

Wayne not only knew he wanted to build a sculpture park. He wanted to earn a living from it. He wanted to be an artist, but he still wanted to eat. So he had to find a way.

"I have no idea how to sell art, but I had a need to make art so that's what I did."

He had to create an art exhibit that visitors would pay admission to see and he had to build it on a budget.

Wayne also had to overcome his lack of worldliness in the art business.

"I was just a guy in a blacksmith shop," he said.

He was the very definition of outsider art in the sense that he was self-taught, had a small following limited to his immediate geographic area, had no gallery representation, and no art world connections of any kind.

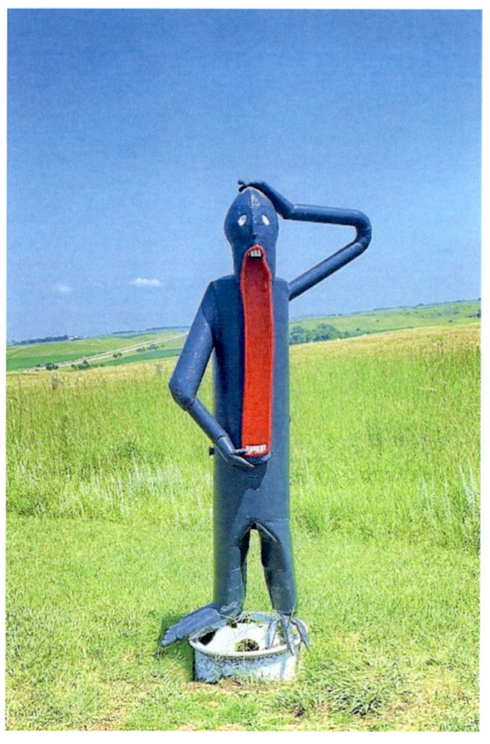

The "Screaming Man" sculpture is based on cartoons Wayne watched as a child where a character's jaw would drop in surprise.

What he had was a collection of sculptures and a dream and he saw no reason why he shouldn't pursue it.

He began to ask people for advice about how to set up his business.

"I talked to everybody," he recalled.

He sought advice from strangers and from people he'd known all his life, finding that people who didn't know anything about the art business knew common sense business skills and could offer him guidance about a fiscally conservative launch.

"I got a lot of good advice from farmers," Wayne said. "Farmers are often good businessmen. They have to anticipate droughts and low prices."

He bounced ideas and concepts off his family, especially his younger brother Ron Porter, who was still in high school at the park's earliest conceptual stage and whom he later immortalized in a sculpture.

Wayne began looking for examples of business plans. He found other sculpture parks, but they were non-profits, some owned by wealthy collectors. He wanted to focus on a for-profit business model.

"There was no business plan to follow," he said.

So he created a plan of his own, starting with his concept.

Wayne knew how he wanted the park to look and the feeling he wanted to convey. He wanted it to be thought-provoking, but fun in a family-friendly setting.

He wanted a plot of land large enough for visitors to take a pleasant walk among the sculptures or take a spin in a golf cart.

He wanted it to be art you can touch.

"The whole object is to make a happiness machine. It's a fun machine. I like the big show. I'd run it like a carnival if I could."

And he knew the setting he wanted.

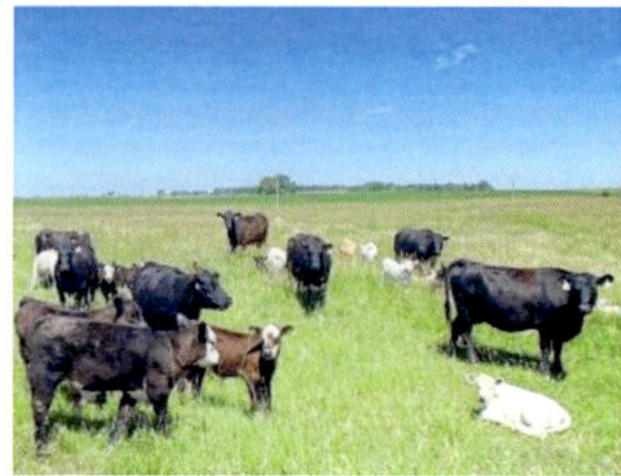
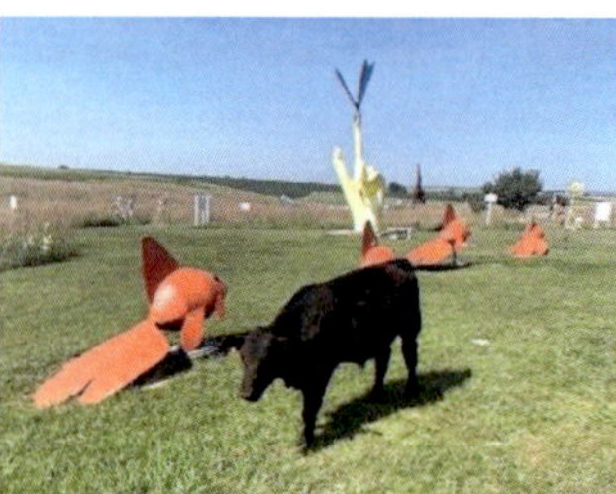

Cattle graze in the sculpture park in the off-season and in the surrounding pastures when the park is open.
Bull calf walking next to sculpture photo courtesy of Wayne Porter

"I wanted a spot with grass and cattle. You can't compete with nature. I wanted a visual site with nature."

With the "what" question answered, he next had to figure out where.

Just as business owners with a storefront consider the amount of foot traffic and street traffic in their business planning, Wayne needed to look for tourist traffic on a highway.

He looked for land in the Black Hills in the western side of the state, home to Mount Rushmore and to the Crazy Horse Memorial, the giants of South

Dakota tourism. But the reality of real estate scarcity in a highly traveled tourist area clouded that vision.

"All the prime real estate is taken," he said. "We couldn't find land out there. There was a rattlesnake infested hill in Wasta. It was a steep hill a golf cart couldn't survive if it was going down."

His brother suggested they look on the eastern side of the state. Wayne considered land in Minnehaha County around Sioux Falls, the state's largest city.

But when he looked at costs, he saw that the land in neighboring McCook County had lower land prices and property taxes. He set his sights on a scenic, eighteen-acre cow pasture along Interstate 90 located near the tiny town of Montrose.

"One guy owned the best pieces of land. I said, 'Ron, we can't call him. He's a big businessman.'"

That didn't deter his brother.

"Ron called Duane Spader and he said, 'That sounds fun!'"

Since start-up money was tight, the established entrepreneur rented the land to the budding art entrepreneur for more than a decade before selling it to him.

Spader says he liked Wayne's concept, plan and determination so much that he let Wayne use a sign that he used for his own business advertising at a cost of "whatever he could afford to pay me."

"I just respected him so much because of his dedication," Spader said.

While farmers around him planted their corn and soybean crops, Wayne Porter began planting his metal sculptures in his picturesque pasture in 2000, seventeen years after he built his first large dragon at his dad's blacksmith shop.

When he saw the effects of nature on his artwork, he knew his careful consideration of a location for the park was worth the time, the effort, and the consternation.

The pastoral prairie setting is an integral part of the customer experience at the park and what Wayne loves about the location. If you ask him what he likes most about the setting, he smiles.

"Just beauty. I see the wind move the grass, the moon, the full moon that lights up the park," he said.

Spectacular sunrises and sunsets play off the sculptures with sunlight streaming through the art, settling into a soft glow behind some of the works, casting shadows and circling as a golden orb around others.

Morphing cloud formations and the ever shifting palette of sky colors serve as a constantly changing natural background for the sculptures, creating newness every day.

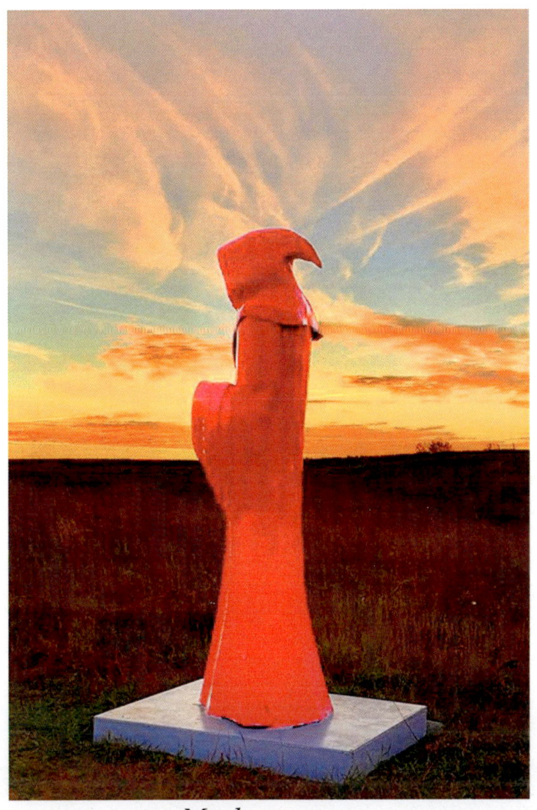

Monk at sunset.
The monk sculptures were inspired by "How the Irish Saved Civilization," a book about monks transcribing Greek and Latin documents to preserve history.

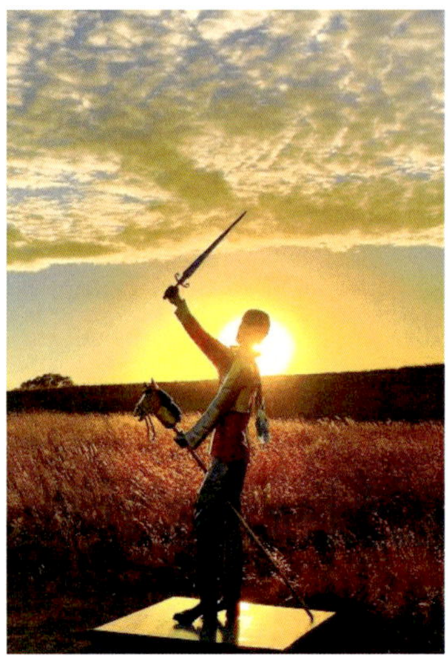

"Purple Ron/Yankee Rider" at sunset

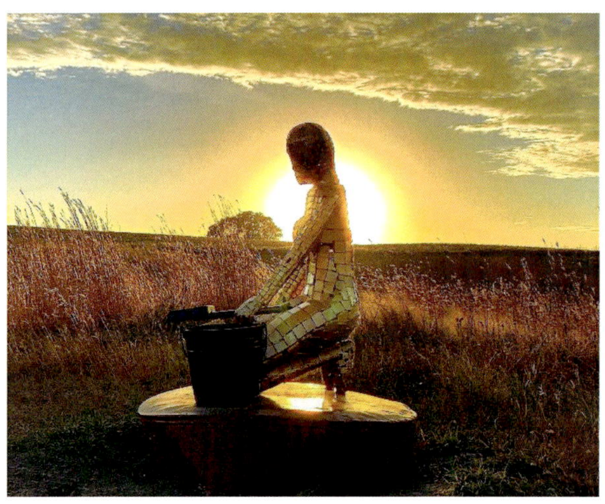

"The Ballerina" at sunset

The lush green grass and wildflowers of spring and summer metamorphosize into the brilliant colors of fall: warm, vibrant shades ranging from straw to gold, orange and red, blending with the sun as though brushed with watercolor.

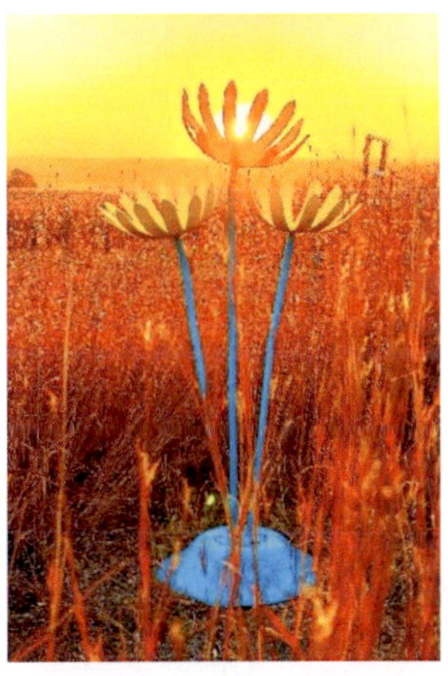

A flower sculpture catches the sunrise amid the colors of fall at Porter Sculpture Park.

In spring, birds build nests in the sculptures and hatch their eggs there.

Wide-eyed little calves frolic in play as their mothers graze in the surrounding pastures. Tiny flickertail gophers scurry around the park searching for seeds and grass to eat.

Coyotes can sometimes be heard yipping in the distance.

The setting is both bucolic and surreal, natural and intentional.

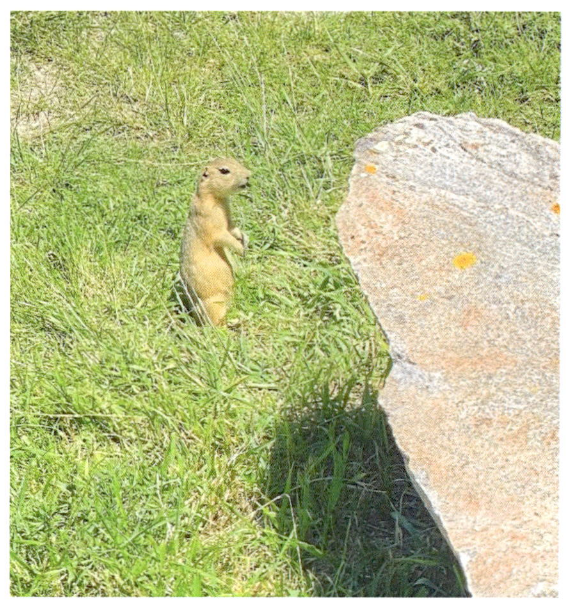

A flickertail gopher standing by a rock. Watching the tiny animals delights visitors as they observe nature at the park.

Porter Sculpture Park is located on a hill, which dips down into a valley along Interstate 90. As you crest the rise before the park and descend into the valley on the interstate, the colorful sculptures provide a head-turning “what’s that” moment.

Just as surrounding farmers cultivated and harvested their traditional crops from their fields, Wayne harvested the interstate. It's a high-traffic location, but in the early years, there were more "what's that" moments from afar than visitors who found their way into the art exhibit.

The sculptures piqued people's interest, but not enough to draw them into the park in large numbers. Some didn't realize it was a sculpture park that was open to the public.

As grazing land for cattle before it was a sculpture park, the location wasn't established as an address, so Wayne sometimes didn't even get his mail.

"Amazon delivered a package to a corn field," he ruefully recalls.

"The early years were slow, very slow. The early years were tough."

The former sheep rancher had sold his sheep to finance the park and the tourist income he'd expected to carry it was far from what he had anticipated.

And, as with any business, there are expenses. The park can be accessed by the interstate, a state highway and a county gravel road, but the road in the park itself was only a path in a cow pasture when he started.

Wayne and his brother brought in bulldozers to build the road, which must be maintained and graveled annually. Sculptures must be painted periodically.

But even though money was scarce, he still had a vision. The artistic entrepreneur always believed that his sculpture park would eventually thrive no matter what obstacles he encountered.

"Entrepreneurs often know so little, they think they can't fail," he said. "I couldn't figure out why it was slow. I stayed with it."

He was also fortunate to have family input and encouragement. His mother and father, retired by the time the park opened, did everything from help move the sculptures to maintain the park, give tours and handle the entrance fees.

His engineer brother Ron provides technical and mechanical support. His sister Audrey is in charge of the marketing and also paints the sculptures at the park.

"The sculpture park is like a family farm," Wayne said. "We have a purpose and we all have different skills."

Audrey has free rein to choose the paint colors, which evolve like the ever-changing landscape and is part of the intended experience at the sculpture park.

"Over the years, the art will be a different color," Wayne explains. "That's part of the art too."

The Porter family has conquered the art of what makes sibling relationships work in a business relationship, where the choice of partners can make or break a venture.

Wayne and Ron are able to disagree without being disagreeable and they have a shared sense of humor.

"We tease each other all the time," Wayne said. "We don't get mad at each other. He knows I want the best for him and he wants the best for me."

His brother Ron adds, "I think the business relationship works great because Wayne and I have been doing everything under the sun together since we were kids and, because of this, we understand each other really well. We know what the other person thinks and why they think that way."

Their relationship is exemplified in an incident that happened when they were young men and Ron visited Wayne's sheep ranch.

Wayne was riding his one horse to check on his flock.

The incident ended in Wayne saving Ron's life when Ron decided to ride another animal: the wrong animal. Wayne displays the story and how it became part of his art in a sign by the sculpture that depicts Ron on a stick horse, writing:

My brother Ron Porter, a co-founder of the sculpture park and I were checking sheep. There was one horse.

"I can ride better than you. I can rope better than you. I am wiser than you. I should be on the horse," Ron said.

I said, "You are on foot."

Later, from the back of the horse, I looked with binoculars in the direction of my brother.

He had roped the wild guard donkey.

Donkeys, like llamas, are used to guard sheep. The donkey was alternately dragging him and trampling him. There was no snubbing post or breaking corral.

I went to help. After great effort and many bruises, we were able to get the rope off.

I said to Ron, "The only equine you should train to ride is a stick horse and I am going to make a monument to that fact."

He said, "Okay, but make me taller."

I made him taller.

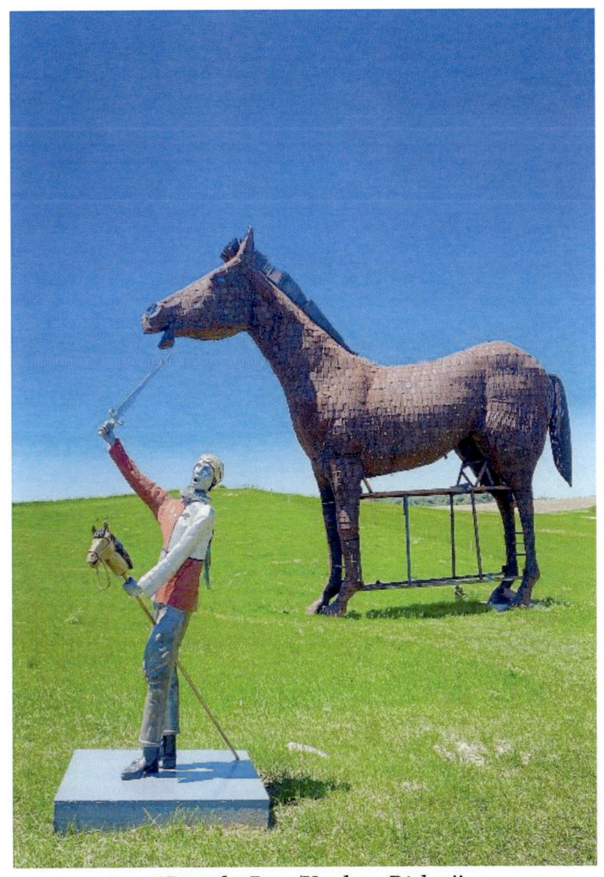

"Purple Ron/Yankee Rider"
depicts Wayne's brother on a stick horse.

With a history of being there for each other, the family shares the same commitment to the park that Wayne does. Like Wayne, they didn't waver in the lean years and they were willing to be flexible if the park hadn't worked in the form they had originally planned.

"I never thought very much about whether the park would make it or not because I knew we would never stop trying to make it work," Ron said. "I always thought if we never stop trying, we could make it work at some level."

Turning Point

In addition to persistence, two other factors were instrumental in the park's success: the bull and increased usage of the internet, which was still a relatively young technology when Wayne started.

He planned the opening of the park around the bull, even though he wouldn't move the massive sculpture to the park until the second year. Although there were fifty sculptures at the opening, he knew the smaller pieces by themselves wouldn't be enough to pull people off the interstate.

Wayne knew that he needed a show-stopper and a traffic stopper. And that's exactly what the bull provided. The bull was his first sculpture of major scale. At sixty feet high, it's as tall as the faces on Mount Rushmore.

Three years before he opened the park, Wayne began work on the bull using 100-year-old steel railroad tie plates, a choice based not only on their recycled historical value, but also on their strength.

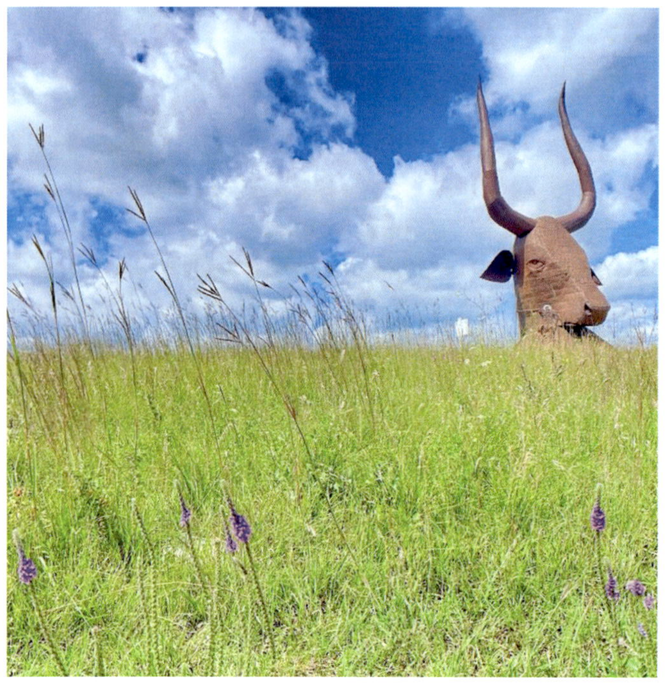

The Bull with vervain wildflowers in the foreground and clouds in the background.

.

"Railroads used the best steel. They didn't want the tracks to break."

At the time, he was making customized crow bars that were tempered to be especially strong for the Dakota Minnesota Eastern Railroad.

Wayne asked to be paid in tie plates instead of money. The railroad provided thousands of the almost ten-pound tie plates in payment.

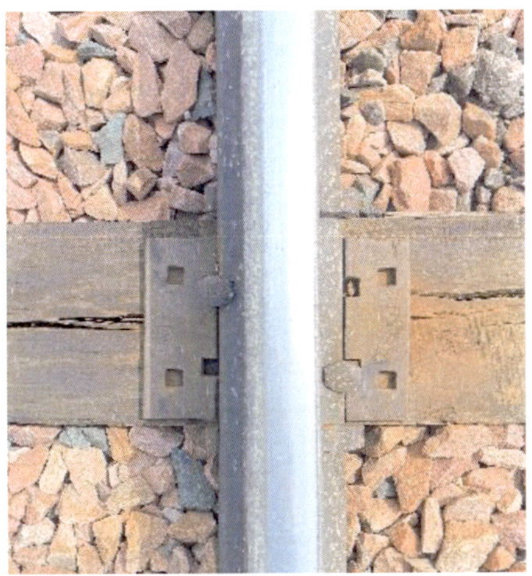

Tie plates are the metal pieces along the rail on railroad tracks.

Wayne heated the dense steel tie plates over hot coals and firewood and manipulated them with a metal press, then welded the pieces together.

He compares it to putting together a jigsaw puzzle. When the pieces didn't fit together as he anticipated, he'd grab another piece of metal or re-work one and re-position it.

He divided the bull into two parts, working on the horns and head separately, so he was welding and working the steel at thirty feet in the air instead of the full sixty feet.

Wayne wasn't mathematically calculating how the two pieces would fit and balance on a work of this scale. He says he's not even good at math.

The artist doesn't make sketches or CAD drawings of his sculptures either.

Wayne compares his technique to a painter who paints entire scenes without drawing first, an ability that is innate in some people.

He measures and calculates in his own way by using his instinctive eye, his many years of experience in metal work, and by sometimes placing smaller items on the parts to use as his own model of sorts.

It's his lack of specific calculations that often amazes park visitors who have building experience.

The task of moving the behemoth 140 miles from his hometown to his sculpture park was a monumental feat as well. Moving the bull called for mechanical engineering expertise, provided by his brother Ron.

"I'm structural," Wayne said. "I'm not mechanical. He's a mechanical engineer."

They hired a crane to load the two 20-ton parts onto two lowboy flatbed trailer trucks.

The crane operator looked at the two massive parts and asked if Wayne had run the numbers to be sure they'd fit together at the sculpture park.

No, he hadn't, but he was sure they'd fit.

The two semi-trucks carried the bull's head and the bull's horns down the highway to the sculpture park so they could be set and secured on concrete. They fit together and balanced perfectly.

As a promotion, the bull did the trick. It is impossible to miss. It is iconic.

But, even though drivers on the interstate saw it, many still didn't make the connection between the bull and an art venue that was open to the public.

"One guy said he kept driving by and didn't know it was a park. He thought it was some rancher's favorite cow that had died and he made a monument to it."

The bull enthusiast couldn't figure out how to get into the park because Wayne only had one sign along the interstate and no signs directing the way. But the fan was determined to learn the story behind the enormous bovine and eventually found his way to the bull in the sculpture park.

As more visitors began to follow, Wayne began to get local news coverage, but it took ten years to get his first big publicity break outside the region.

The bull caught the eye of *Time Magazine* and the park was featured in a story about the nation's top roadside attractions.

A *Boston Globe* story was next after the reporter drove by on the interstate, spotted the bull, and wrote a story.

That's when Wayne saw his first sign of success. His website crashed from all the new traffic.

Other coverage followed until he was seen in publications and media outlets from coast to coast and around the world. Travel websites and social media were other milestones that ramped up exposure.

Visitors and profits increased from a trickle to a flow, and eventually, to a steady stream of sightseers from all over the nation and the world.

Finally, Wayne was making a profit as he intended: not by selling his sculptures, but by sharing them with the world at his sculpture park.

Above the Dark Side

As much as the bull was a boon to business, it was also Wayne's introduction to fame's dark side.

In addition to admirers, the bull head also attracted the attention of some detractors.

They saw the horns as ominous and misinterpreted a smaller sculpture he placed inside the bull as sinister.

In 2023, someone vandalized the bull and stole the ram heads of the guardian sculptures he built to surround the bull.

In doing so, they didn't just steal Wayne's physical property and intellectual property.

The perpetrators had also stolen and damaged three years of work. That's how long it had taken Wayne to make all the ram sculptures.

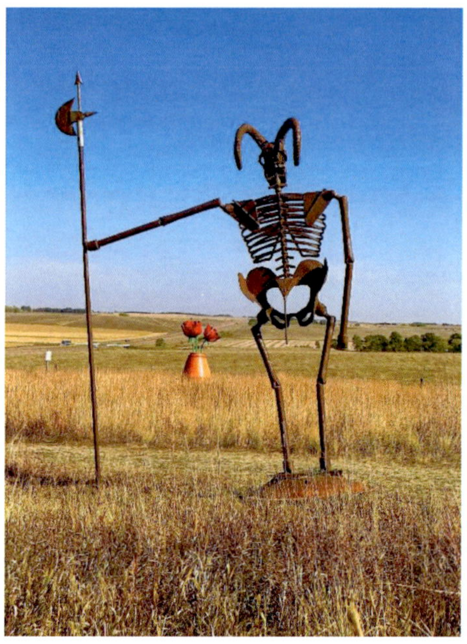

One of the Guardian Ram sculptures that surround the bull

Wayne intellectualizes the theft with his usual optimism, saying that the perpetrators just didn't understand the sculptures and didn't ask about the meaning.

"People bring their own brains. Some people find some dark. But it depends on their perception."

The thieves' perception of Wayne's intentions is completely inaccurate.

"I'm very spiritual," he said. "Most artists are."

Wayne grew up as a Catholic boy from cattle county, where, as he says, "Cows outnumber people thirty to one." He lived on his family's farm for four years before his father decided a career as a blacksmith was more stable for his wife and five children.

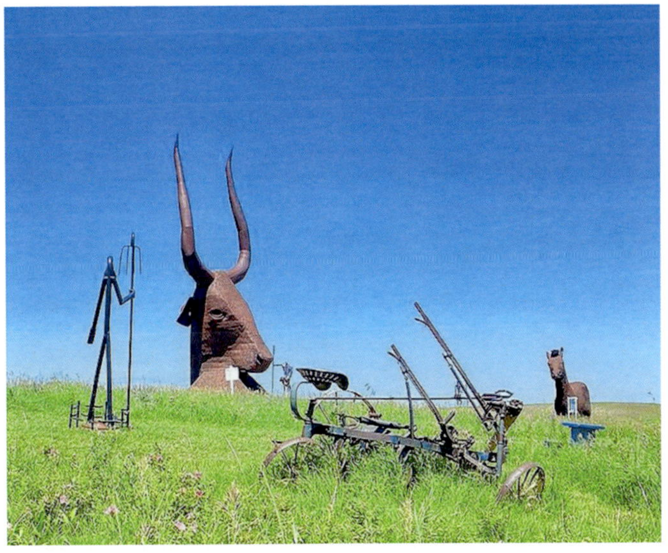

Wayne displays some farm equipment among the sculptures, including a plow from his great grandfather's era that was pulled by horse or oxen.

While on the farm, Wayne was fascinated by the family's bulls, which he describes as one having a nice deposition and one as mean and threatening. He was taught to respect them from a distance.

He enjoyed reading books about animals and history, including a particularly influential book he remembers from fifth grade that had vibrant artwork of an aqua colored bull. Now, he thinks it was based on Minoan bull art.

At that time, he didn't know anything about the Minoans, their reverence for bulls and their vivid depiction of bulls in art on everything from frescoes to palaces, but the use of unexpected colors on a bull fixated him.

As an adult educated in history, he based the shape of his bull's horns on ancient Egyptian longhorn cattle revered in antiquity and art for their sheer raw strength and bulk.

"The bull is always part of history. The power and the energy of the bull is always fascinating."

"The Egyptians saw the bull as a symbol of strength and fertility. It's seen as a symbol of leadership and authority, untamed power and awe and respect," Wayne explains.

The face of the bull resembles the modern Hereford cattle he saw in South Dakota mixed with Braham influences within the Egyptian stylization, making his bull sculpture his own form of hybrid, a figurative cross-breeding of cattle in metal form.

"It's Egyptian history meshing with Hand County."

The sculptures Wayne placed inside the bull head that are accessible through a back entrance were an after-thought, added between the period when the bull was finished and when it was moved.

"I was just having so much fun that I kept adding to it."

He sculpted serpents, spiders and a colony of bats to hang from the beams and walls as *Indiana Jones* style obstacles. He placed a hammer inside to look as though he had unintentionally dropped it.

He paid tribute to movies he liked as a child. Witch's legs are a nod to the *Wizard of Oz*.

A sculpture perched on the interior wall by the bull's nose is based on his memories of another of his childhood favorites, the 1950's monster movie, *The Creature from the Black Lagoon*.

"I just made a little movie set inside," he explained.

Another Behemoth

His second massive sculpture was a horse that stands forty feet tall by fifty feet long.

Wayne kept it in the same style as the bull, again using railroad tie plates. This time he used heavier thirty pound railroad tie plates that he purchased from a scrap yard in Watertown, South Dakota.

The horse was a more complicated project than the bull, in part, because it stands on long, slender legs instead of a broad base like the bull. That changes the balance requirements.

"The bull only took three years. That impresses me after working on the horse. That horse kicked me around for ten cold winters."

Mishaps can be part of any construction project and the horse was no exception.

As he welded inside the belly of the horse, sparks frequently set fire to his coat. He sometimes batted out the flames with one hand and used his other hand to douse them with the iced tea he usually drinks.

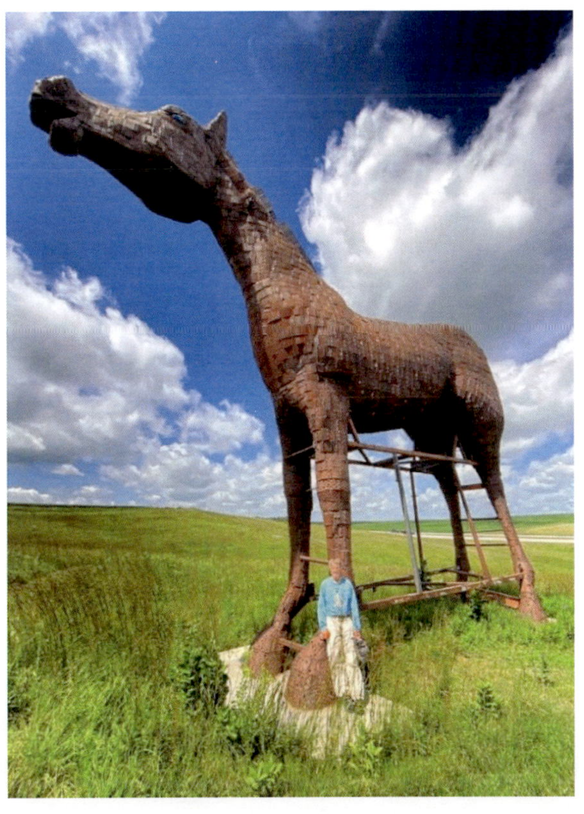

Wayne standing by a horse hoof shows the scale of the horse.

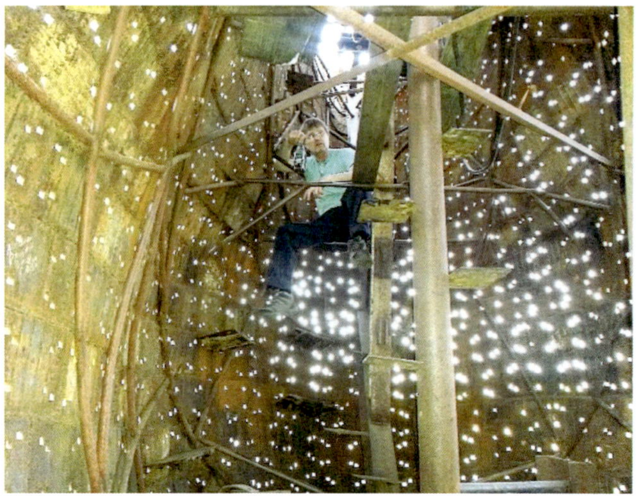

Wayne working inside the belly of the horse.

One cold winter evening, he dropped his favorite hammer into the horse's narrow leg and climbed down to retrieve it only to realize that he couldn't get out.

"I was like a kid falling into a well. I thought, no one will hear me scream."

His nearest neighbor had already walked her dog for the night and wouldn't take out her pet for another walk until morning.

Facing the prospect of a long night in freezing temperatures, upside down and stuck in quarters too tight to allow him to push with his legs, Wayne wedged his arms against the sides of the horse's leg and slowly and painfully began trying to claw and inch himself up with his fingers and hands.

"It had to work," he said.

Wayne knew that if he couldn't get himself out on the first attempt, the situation would turn even more dire because he would eventually become too cold, too numb and too exhausted to keep trying.

He emerged tired and shaken with aching hands and arms and, amazingly, the hammer.

While the bull was built in two pieces, Wayne constructed the horse in one piece in his hometown, then removed the top part to move it as two separate pieces when it was time to take it to the sculpture park, again another delicate feat of engineering.

The horse was more expensive to move than the bull. Even though the weights of the two are similar, the weight distribution was different because the horse was longer than it is tall and balanced on its long legs.

"The horse was just a different animal," Wayne explained.

The top half had to be detached and lifted off the bottom half by a ten-wheel drive, 200-ton crane, which was heavier and bigger than the crane required for the bull. The cost of the crane added up to $1000 an hour over three days.

Then there was the expense of hiring two cargo semi-trucks to haul the two parts to his sculpture park to be re-assembled there.

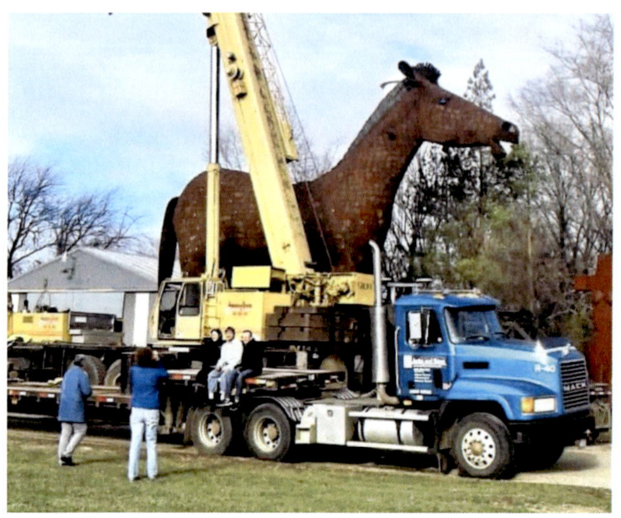

Audrey, Wayne and Ron Porter on the moving truck in 2018. The horse towers above at treetop level.

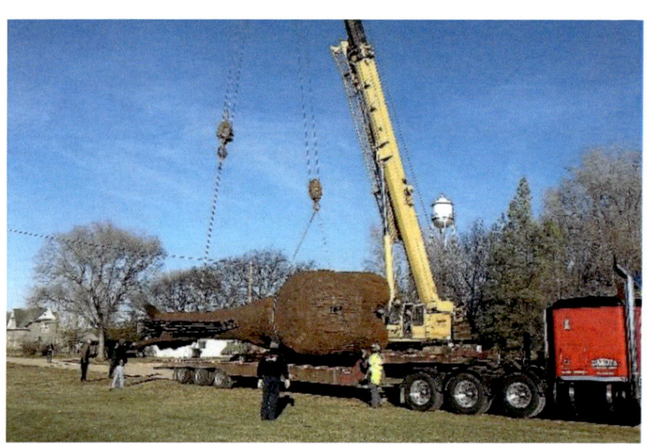

A 200-ton crane placed both parts of the horse on two flatbed trucks for the move to the sculpture park.

By this time in 2018, Wayne was well known enough to get funding help from friends and fans.

His sister Audrey launched an internet-based crowd-funding campaign, which offered contributors commemorative coffee cups featuring the horse.

The campaign yielded $16,000, enough to balance the rest of the costs, which were covered by Wayne and his family.

The biggest percentage of contributions came from those who know him best in McCook County, where the park is based, and his home base of Hand County, where some contributors still proudly display their horse cups.

Today, the horse stands facing the bull as a giant, double tribute to not only his own fascination with animals and his farming and ranching background, but also to one of the primary occupations of the state where he lives.

Facing the Future

Wayne sometimes thinks about concentrating on only smaller sculptures. Small for him is still big, though. Even as he made that statement, he was working on a thirty foot rabbit.

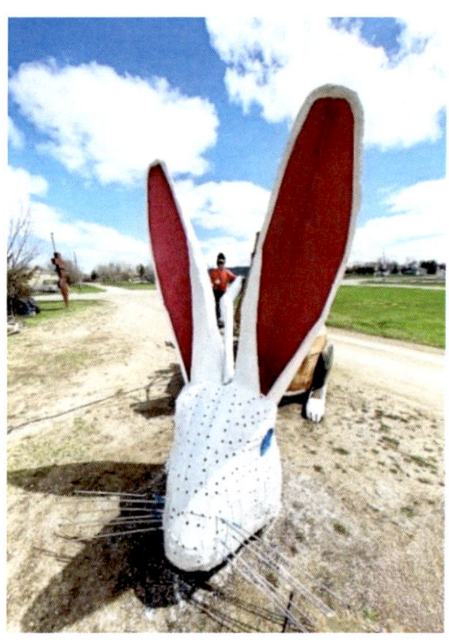

Wayne working on the rabbit's head

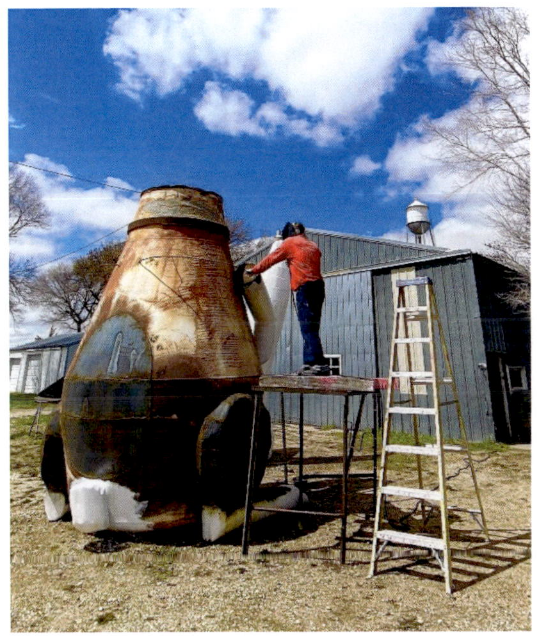

Wayne working on the rabbit at his shop.
The body is a cement mixer bowl.
The head is made of the same railroad
tie plates he used for the bull and horse.

The sculpture is based on the white rabbit in another of his favorite childhood books, "Alice's Adventures in Wonderland," a fictional fantasy classic written by Lewis Carroll.

Wayne's "White Rabbit" is inscribed with some quotations from the book as well as mathematical equations, adding an element of logic to Alice's Wonderland, where many characters were frenzied and life in Wonderland became more and more bizarre or "curiouser and curiouser" as Alice described it.

Why the combination of fantasy and logic by adding math on a sculpture? Wayne believes they have much in common at their base. "Art and science," he said. "It's about curiosity."

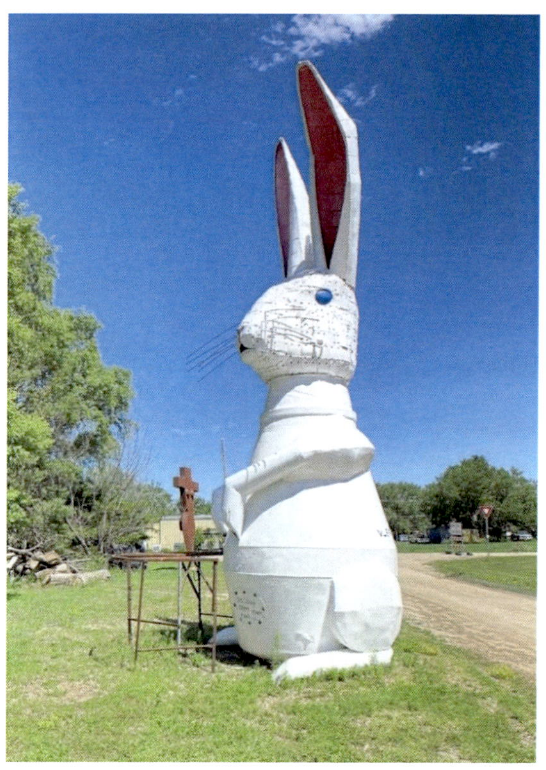

The White Rabbit at Wayne's shop

His decision to consider taking a break from massive projects and confine his art to sculptures around thirty feet or less is based on pragmatic considerations.

Not only are they all-consuming, but he has less time to work on them. His park's popularity led him to extend his tourist season, which shortened his off-season sculpting time in the late fall, winter and early spring weather.

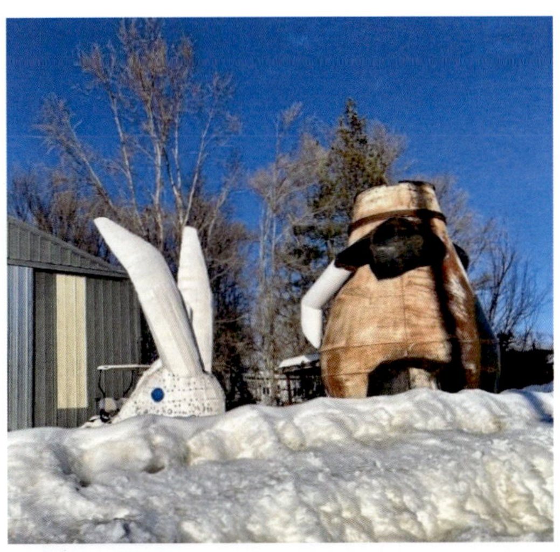

Wayne works on his sculptures at his shop during the park's off-season, including during the snowy winter months.

As he entered his 60’s, he began to find winter temperatures that can dip well below freezing less tolerable, which is why he began to think about putting off massive pieces at least until he can build a warmer shop. Or, perhaps, or until inspiration overtakes him and he builds another large piece anyway.

It may be somewhat of a change of course, but also an opportunity to spend more time on other artistic endeavors.

I'm an ordinary man.
I live ordinary days.
It's ordinary things that
I have learned to praise.

Wayne Porter
from his poem
"Ordinary Man"

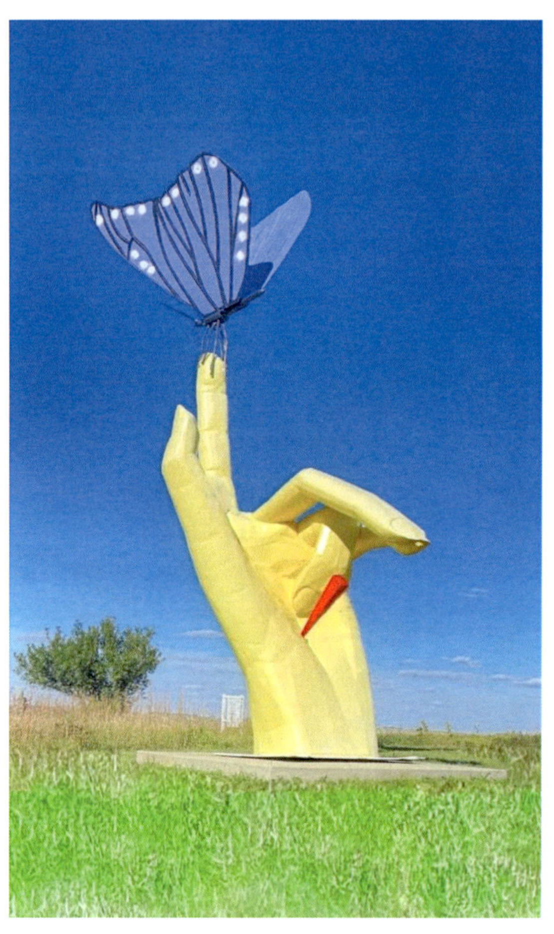

"The Hand and the Butterfly" sculpture represents the joy and pain of life.

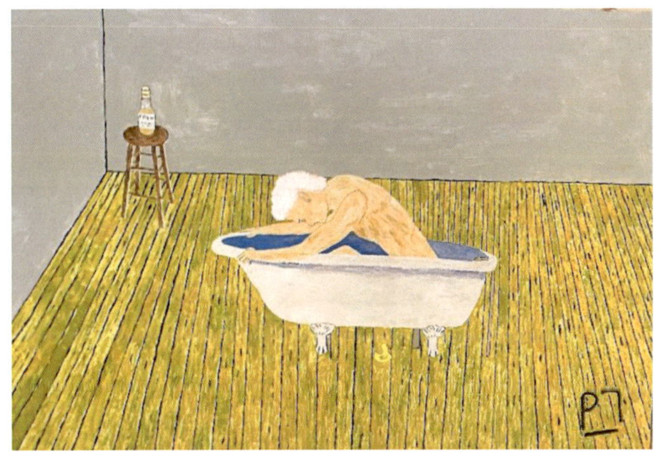

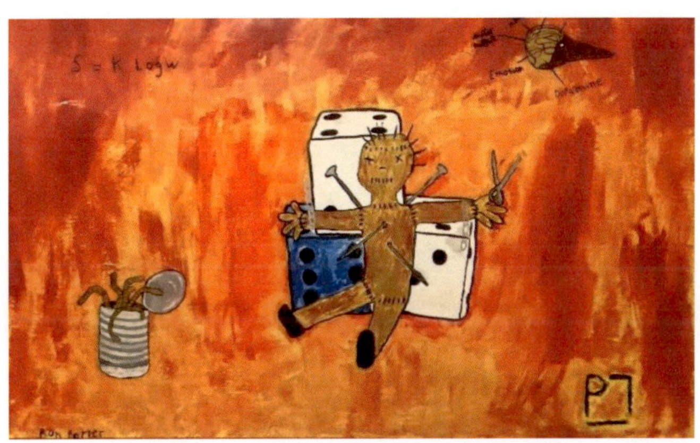

Two of Wayne Porter's paintings.
The top painting is about despair and the
bottom painting is about perceptions of free will.

New Journeys

Creativity seldom limits itself.

In addition to sculpting, Wayne also writes poetry and paints, although painting is secondary and outside his comfort zone.

He insists he's not a good painter, even though his work suggests otherwise.

He has signed paintings with his family's brand instead of his name and even has jokingly signed his brother Ron's name to his paintings because he didn't want to acknowledge the works.

It's an understandable response to the pressure one can feel as an expert in one genre trying his hand at another.

He's comfortable enough as a poet to not only display his work on signs at the sculpture park, but to publish a book of his poetry.

His poems reveal a deeper side as opposed to that of the outwardly affable and gregarious artist who likes to crack jokes and whose philosophy includes a central belief that part of the purpose of life is to enjoy it.

Wayne's interest in poetry was sparked by an inspiring and enthusiastic English teacher at Miller High School when he was a teenager.

"I fell in love with poetry in Mrs. (Beryl) Kelly's class in high school. It just hit me. I like the words. I like the sound of words. I like to play with words."

While he was reading epic poems in English literature and reading poetry books at the library, he wrote his first poem about his little sister Kathy's beginning attempts at cooking, a poem with both a serious tone and a humorous ending.

"I wanted the world to know," he jokes. "Don't eat my sister's meat loaf. It glows in the dark."

It's also a reminder that anything can serve as inspiration.

Much of his poetry allows him to share his feelings about life and its unanswered questions, about why people think the way they think, and to pontificate about the world, the universe and our place in it, even down to the particles that make up matter and objects.

"Reality is in the nature of the particles and the arrangement. I keep thinking everything is made by something else. People don't think of it. I think of it too much and then I have to explain to the world. But I suppose that's what artists do."

His sister Kathy inspired two more works when she and Wayne were reminiscing about a goldfish aquarium they owned as children.

His brother David found a baby bullhead fish in Turtle Creek and decided it would be a good addition to their fish family in the aquarium, but the bullhead didn't agree.

Not wanting to be confined, the baby bullhead repeatedly jumped out of the goldfish bowl.

Wayne saw symbolism in that.

Years later, he not only created a sculpture with leaping fish, but also wrote a poem about fish trying to escape from a goldfish bowl just as his baby bullhead had leapt from a bowl that was sized for goldfish, a bowl too small to contain a fish designed for greater waters.

In addition to representing one very determined bullhead, Wayne says the sculpture represents the desire to go beyond your confines to explore and to acquire more knowledge.

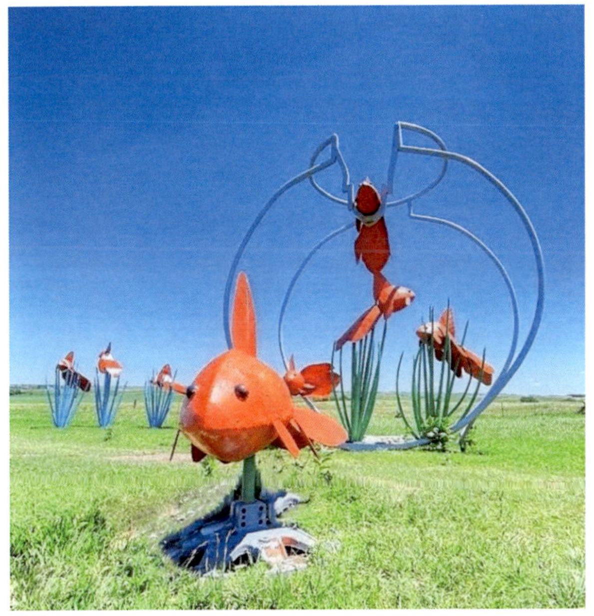

"The Goldfish Bowl"

"Looking for King Kong" is about life's unpredictability and being at the mercy of the universe.

Wayne wrote "The Hammer" as a tribute to his father and as an acknowledgement of his own lack of permanence.

He also wrote about his initial rejection of his artistic life course, his obsession with art, his efforts to shake his driving desire to create (which he called the beast), and his eventual happy acceptance of his life as an artist in a poem named "Feeding the Beast."

Feeding the Beast
by Wayne Porter

I heard the voice of the beast.
Serve me,
He said.

I will not serve you
I said

Soon, he spoke again
Serve me
Said the beast

What will you give me?
I asked

Hunger, rags and humiliation
said the beast

I will not serve you
I said

His shadow followed me
I would glimpse him
from the corner of my eye

He haunted me

Hammer for me a trinket
And I will leave you
Said the beast

I hammered him a trinket
I tossed it at his feet
Leave me
I said

Just one more and I will leave
Perhaps a poem
said the beast

That was long ago

I now serve at the feet of the beast
I feed the beast
and beg for his crumbs.

Some of his poems are interspersed with the sculptures at the park, adding interpretation and meaning to the works.

He also displays a poem his mother wrote about her observations of life and death and spirituality during her nursing career.

Wayne has written about what motivates him, his purpose and his passion and about why he and other artists create.

"All art is the truth. The compulsion to do art is about telling the truth. They don't do it to get rich and famous."

He wrote "The Wild Ride" while building his giant horse. While he wasn't consciously writing about himself when he penned it, the poem nevertheless represents his own journey and the tenacity it took to pursue his dream, a gutsy goal for an untrained artist living in a small town.

"There are always artists in a small town," he said. "They just don't display their work."

"I just never stopped. The ones who don't stop are the ones we call artists."

In the beginning, he was driven by his obsession to create. Later, he found that purpose as much or more than passion is his driving force: a purpose to share his creative world with the public and to stimulate conversation and contemplation.

The satisfaction he feels when visitors appreciate his creativity and talk to him about his work allows him to transcend the cold days in winter when he swings his hammer and wields his welding torch, and to put in perspective how he arrived where he is today doing what he loves.

If you ask him if sculpting feels like work to him, Wayne takes a moment to think about how to answer a question about a passion that is also his vocation.

"You're dedicated and put in a lot of hours. Okay. It's work," he concedes.

His poem that he named "The Wild Ride" is an acknowledgement of that labor of love and the embodiment of the journey that has taken him to exactly where he wanted to be.

It represents the path he crafted, the initial self-doubt he had to overcome to believe he could make a living from art, the determination and perseverance he demonstrated when he realized that his dream was possible, and what he learned along the way.

"The horse is a metaphor. When you're young, you have this 'I can take over the world, I can do anything' mentality. When you're older and wiser, you have a different viewpoint on life. It's a wild ride. And the thing is, when you cross the finish line, you have a smile on your face and you're the winner then."

The Wild Ride

by Wayne Porter

The reckless and bold with flowing manes
burst from the gate
no time to wait
Hold tight to the reins

A steed gains with sides
heaving, heaving, heaving
with time leaving

No place to hide
It's a wild ride
Hold tight to the reins

With what time remains, hearts are
beating, beating, beating
with moments fleeting

We have never the time we need
to reign in a fierce steed
Hold tight to the reins

With the wind in your hair
breathe the night air
Cherish your scars
dream of the stars
almost there.

The cautious and wise end the race
at a slower pace.
When the race is done
all bow to the setting sun
The winners of the race
are those with a smile
across their face.

Wayne wrote the poem "Perfect World" when he was working on the "The Hand and the Butterfly," a twelve-foot-tall hand holding a butterfly on its finger with a thorn piercing the palm.

It's a visual commentary on the joy and pain of life, which included a broken arm when a piece of metal fell on him as he was working on the sculpture.

He displays a sign at his sculpture park explaining that "Pain and joy can co-exist, but neither stays forever. Butterflies fly away. Thorns are pulled."

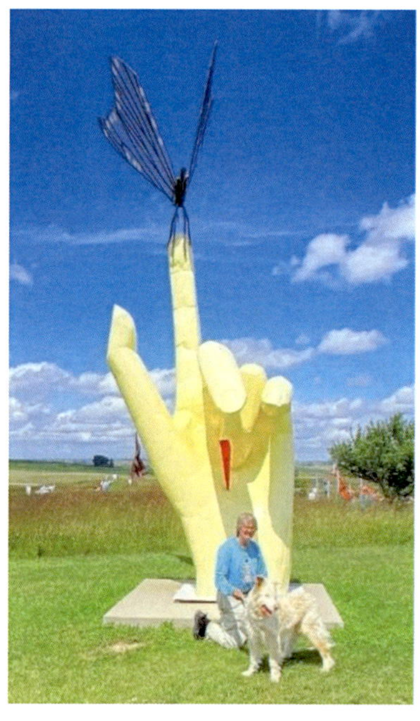

Wayne and his pet Bambino. The dog was a happy greeter at the park for almost 15 years.

His poem "Perfect World" is also about the importance of finding what's worthwhile in life and being open to it.

"It's just talking about how brief life is and that everything dies. We lose people and that's just how life is. So you grab what beauty you can. That's the theme of life. It's everywhere if you just notice it."

And even though he didn't intend it as first, the poem is also a thoughtful summarization of the escape that he shares with the world in the natural and peaceful setting of his sculpture park and of a life spent searching for and creating color, form, beauty and meaning.

Perfect World
by Wayne Porter

I promise you a perfect world
beneath the patterns of the colored sky
as if this world were never here.

Eternity has gone away
with nothing left on earth to say
and it never mattered anyway.

Somewhere in between
what is and what may seem
we can hold the perfect world
perhaps in a dream.

Let the bones of the prophets turn to dust.
I offer you this perfect world
but if it can't be, then let us die
beneath the patterns of a colored sky.

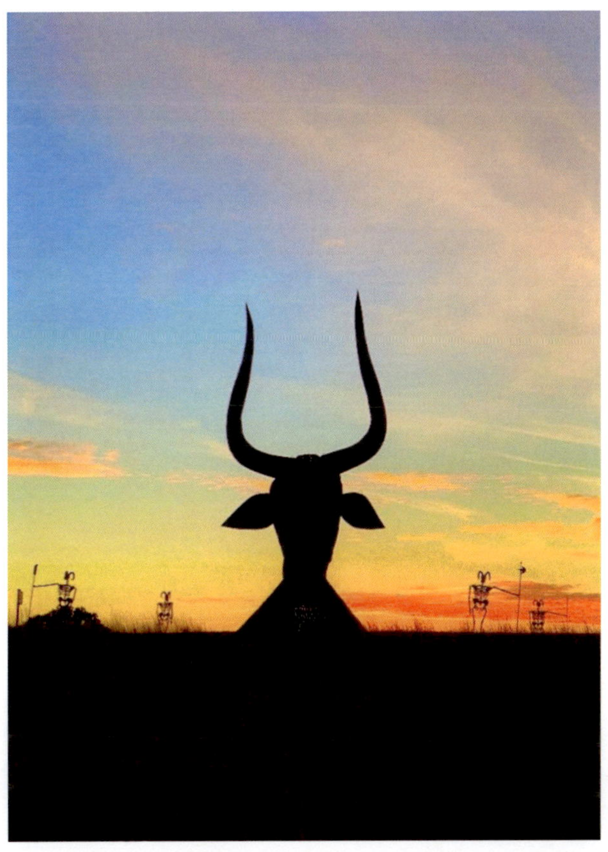

Give me
The bird as it sings
The wind through the rye
The stars in the sky
Give me
Ordinary Things

Wayne Porter
from his poem
"Ordinary Man"

Art Analysis, Impact and Author's Note

The Wayne Effect

With visitors from all over the nation and the world who seek out his sculpture park, Wayne Porter makes a significant contribution to the public art scene and especially to a contemporary direction.

When he opened his park in 2000, he was at the cusp of an expanding art scene in South Dakota. The Washington Pavillion had just opened in Sioux Falls. Renown wildlife artist Terry Redlin's Art Center in Watertown had opened three years earlier.

All followed the South Dakota Art Museum, which originally was built to display Harvey Dunn's homestead paintings in 1970 and was expanded in 2002. Rapid City's Dahl Arts Center was also built in the 1970's.

The historic Corn Palace in Mitchell, which also is an events venue and sports arena, displays murals made of corn on the outside. Inside, it houses some native and Dakota Modern works of artist Oscar Howe, who designed many corn murals in the past.

Wayne's art took the next step in both style and in visibility. He brought "what's that" to the forefront.

And he did it as an individual artist without an organization or foundation behind him.

His location on a busy interstate highway puts him front and center in South Dakota's tourism traffic and in a position to contribute further to promote the state's art scene. Wayne is supportive of other artists and suggests other art venues that tourists can visit as they continue their travels.

"All art has the potential to add value to life," said Erik Ritter, an instructor at South Dakota State University. "The park is a great addition to South Dakota public art."

Ritter assigns an official description of Wayne's work as reclaimed surrealist assemblages. Others say his work brings in elements of folk art as well as industrial art. Whatever they call the sculptures, people respond to them for a multitude of reasons.

"Wayne Porter's sculptures are very creative and playful. They are very personal responses to the world," said John Peters, the coordinator of the Eide Dalrymple Gallery and an instructor at Augustana University. "It's a great example of someone expressing himself," he said. "I call this a must-see site."

"It's a little Wonderland out there," says Amy Fill, the director of the University of South Dakota Art Museum. "There's sense of whimsey and being accessible."

"They're fun. They're silly. They're so free," she said. "But a lot of these are serious pieces."

Porter Sculpture Park is thirty minutes to one hour away from several of the state's universities, providing an example and inspiration for both art students and for other people who might have been hesitant to consider art.

"He may be more of an inspiration to non-art majors and for people when they see what is possible," said Peters.

Amy Fill said Wayne's method of securing thousands of railroad tie plates for the bull by asking the Dakota Minnesota Eastern Railroad to pay him in tie plates instead of money is a good example of ingenuity, as is his recycling of other people's trash.

"He's willing to play with found material, which is inspiring to students when they're working on a budget," she said. "Resources cost money."

And then there's the way he started. That sheer audacity. That relentless drive and unwavering belief of a self-taught artist with no art world connections to try and to keep trying.

He may have been, as he describes himself, "just a guy in a blacksmith shop," but he was the guy who did it against the odds.

"I was really impressed by the ambition he has," said John Peters.

"To just start and be fearless," says Amy Fill. "That's the first step."

Author's Note

I sometimes wonder if I would have written this book if I hadn't been an insider turned outsider and then turned back to the world I had left behind.

I returned to my home state to help and be with my elderly parents in their final years. Coming back to my childhood home for several years allowed me to see the community and its people with a different perspective.

It also allowed me to take a fresh look at Wayne and his art.

Wayne and I grew up in the same community, meeting when we were about four or five-years-old when his mother was my babysitter.

We played in his backyard along Turtle Creek, oblivious to how our lives would diverge and then later converge again to create this book.

When I left South Dakota after college at SDSU, my life became the fast-paced world of news as a writer and editor at an international news service and then as a television reporter.

As a child, I began to learn about culture by looking at my mother's art appreciation books from her college classes. I was thrilled when my parents took me to see the Harvey Dunn exhibit when it opened, my first in-person viewing of a painter who was known nationally. Up to that point, my museum visits had been largely limited to historical and natural history exhibits in the state.

Later, I developed a further appreciation of art by visiting the nation's most prominent museums and attending lectures while living in, working in, and visiting America's largest cities.

Eventually, I began painting my own art, which gave me insight into the processes of art and an even greater respect for Wayne's talent.

Every time I returned to South Dakota to visit family, my mother and father and brother took me to the blacksmith shop or to the sculpture park to see Wayne's latest projects.

I saw the early works that sat by the street in St. Lawrence for 17 years before they were moved to the sculpture park.

I saw the bull at the shop and watched Wayne work inside the belly of the horse during the construction phase and saw his joyful enthusiasm while wielding his welding tools.

But you don't really know someone until you write a book about him, until you delve into the "how" and the "why" behind the "what."

What I found to be almost as impressive as his art was the extent of the long-term strategizing that went into the sculpture park. Wayne had a plan and worked toward it, keeping his day job of sheep ranching and blacksmithing, and then taking a short-term job at a box factory to make extra money the winter before he opened his park.

This book is based on multiple conversations and official interviews with Wayne over several years and from the perspective of shared memories of the community of our childhood.

My photographs are the result of numerous trips to the sculpture park looking for the perfect lighting to show his sculptures at their best and communicate symbolism. I also used some old photos I had taken over the years when I returned home to visit my family.

My thanks to Wayne for providing the personal pictures of him and his family.

I'm grateful to Wayne for his time and patience for my endless questions for accuracy, context and interpretation of his works. I'm grateful for his friendship, and I'm also grateful that he allowed me to be part of his journey by writing this book.

About the Author

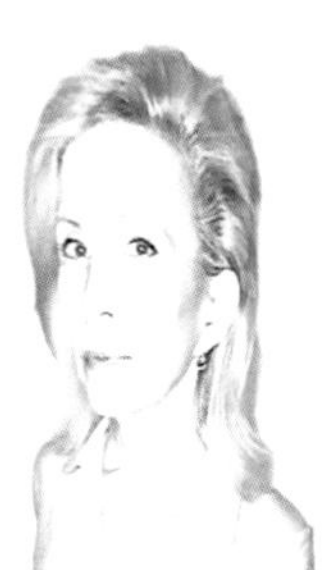

Sue Speck is an award-winning journalist, photographer and artist who has worked for an international news service in Chicago and has worked as a television reporter in Houston, Texas.

A Word about Art

Part of the beauty of art is that it takes two. One to create the work and one to view the work.

The final product becomes a blend of both the artist's intention and the viewer's personal interpretation. This book explains Wayne Porter's intent and his own original interpretation of his work, but your viewpoint is equally as important.

Wayne believes that art is a diary of where the artist was at the time. The way the viewers see it is also a diary of where they are in their lives.

Your interpretation of a work of art (and the artist's interpretation) can change over the years as different experiences in your life lend themselves to new perceptions.

And that's another aspect of the beauty of art. It can grow with you.

Notes and References

Poetry:

P. 35 Wayne Porter, "American Gothic – Shepherd's Dream," "The Poetry of Art"

P. 43 Wayne Porter, "The Daydreamers," "The Poetry of Art"

P. 84, 102 Wayne Porter, "Ordinary Man," "The Poetry of Art"

P. 91 Wayne Porter, "Feeding the Beast," "The Poetry of Art"

P. 45, 95 Wayne Porter, "The Wild Ride," "The Poetry of Art"

P. 99 Wayne Porter, "Perfect World," "The Poetry of Art"

Literary and Historical References

P. 23 John Pickrell, "A T.Rex could have Crushed a Car. Here's How," National Geographic, Sept. 25, 2019.

P. 31 Iowa Public Broadcasting, "The Farm Crisis of the 1980's," 2013

P. 52 Thomas Cahill, "How the Irish Saved Civilization: The Untold Story of Ireland's Heroic Role from the Fall of Rome to the Rise of Medieval Europe." 1995 1st Edition

P. 71 Robert Ballard with Toni Eugene, "Mystery of the Ancient Seafarers, Early Maritime Civilizations," Pages 128-135. 2004

P. 81 Lewis Carroll, "Alice's Adventures in Wonderland" Page 16. Reprint from the original 1886 edition.

Sculpture Index

www.ingramcontent.com/pod-product-compliance
Ingram Content Group UK Ltd.
Pitfield, Milton Keynes, MK11 3LW, UK
UKRC031052310726
14090UKWH00028B/474